Confessions of an Accidental Zoo Curator

Such a pleasure
to have you at my launch
Esther

Annette L. Beckford

Confessions of an Accidental Zoo Curator

By Annette Libeskind Berkovits

Foreword by Lee Ehmke
Director and CEO, Houston Zoo
President, World Association of Zoos and Aquariums
(WAZA), 2013-2015

Tenth Planet Press

First Edition

Paperback ISBN: 978-0- 9987578-0- 3

Kindle ISBN: 978-0- 9987578-1- 0

I dedicate this book to Michael, Camille, and Carmen, with the fondest hope that they and their descendants will be able to enjoy the wonders of nature in environments near and far.

The beauty and genius of a work of art may be reconceived, though its first material expression be destroyed; a vanished harmony may yet again inspire the composer, but when the last individual of a race of living things breathes no more, another heaven and another earth must pass before such a one can be again.

William Beebe,
American Naturalist (1877-1962)

TABLE OF CONTENTS

Foreword

Lee Ehmke
Director and CEO, Houston Zoo
President, World Association of Zoos and Aquariums
(WAZA), 2013-2015

There was a time when most of the books one might find about zoos were written by "animal people"—typically male—often zookeepers or veterinarians. In the past century, the work of zoos was largely conducted by men who were the collectors, the curators, and the caregivers of the wild animals assembled for the amusement, edification, and occasional enlightenment of visitors.

But over the decades, a combination of social forces has resulted in a very different kind of zoo, largely in response to the enormous changes being wrought on our planet and an emerging understanding of the huge responsibility we must assume for the wise stewardship of animals and the natural world. Today's zoos and aquariums, working in concert and united under the umbrella of the World Association of Zoos and Aquariums, are now among the foremost players in the movement to save wildlife and wild places.

Through conservation breeding programs, by conducting and supporting field conservation efforts, and most importantly by providing a window on wild animals to more than 800 million people each year, the collective work of progressive zoos and aquariums worldwide is truly making a difference. The transition from being mere animal showcases to being conservation-driven institutions is still incomplete, but it is well underway. Many species owe their continued existence on our planet to the work of zoos, and direct financial investment in field conservation provided by the zoo community now exceeds $350 million a year. And there is strong evidence that the very act of visiting a good zoo can promote public awareness and concern for the planet's biodiversity, at a time when other forces are increasingly distancing people from direct experience and engagement with the natural world.

One result of this sea change in the purpose and mission of zoos has been a radical shift in the mix of people who work in the field. In the past, zoologists and veterinarians at the top and a workforce of strong and sturdy animal keepers with agrarian backgrounds—predominantly all men—ran and operated zoos around the world. Today's zoo and aquarium personnel are much more likely to be professional, urban, and as often as not, female. As the field has matured and become more sophisticated, teachers, communications specialists, business managers, designers, ethologists, technology experts, psychologists, and artists are as likely to be part of a major zoo or aquarium's staff as zoological curators, animal keepers, and veterinarians. I can think of no one who better represents this huge philosophical and demographic shift than Annette Berkovits. As she colorfully describes in some of this book's vignettes, Annette arrived at a Bronx Zoo that was world–renowned but also a very traditional and change-resistant institution. Her vision, persistence, sheer determination, and good humor—all in evidence in her amazing and amusing stories—allowed her to succeed in ways that are profound and lasting. Upon Annette's retirement from the Wildlife Conservation Society in 2007, she could look back at a very different, much more diverse, and measurably more effective organization.

Annette Berkovits built what was arguably the most progressive and influential zoo-based environmental education program in the world, headquartered at the Bronx Zoo but eventually reaching 49 states (one of the Dakotas being the lone holdout!), and as far away as China, Kenya, and Papua New Guinea. The critical role zoos can play in reaching audiences that will influence the future of wildlife on our planet—whether city residents previously estranged from nature by their urban environments or citizens of emerging nations struggling to eke out a modest lifestyle by utilizing natural resources—was fully leveraged by Annette, her team, and her global colleagues. As a founding member and one-time President of the International Association of Zoo Educators (IZE), Annette was instrumental in facilitating the emergence of conservation education as a hallmark mission of modern zoos and aquariums.

I was privileged to work alongside Annette for some of her most fruitful years at the Wildlife Conservation Society, where she was widely admired and respected. Her commitment to excellence and dedication to the dual causes of enriching peoples' lives and helping to secure a future for wildlife were always evident. The legacy of her work is alive and well in the award-winning exhibits at the Bronx Zoo, in classrooms throughout New York City, in the high-level decisions made by the Wildlife Conservation Society's trustees, and in the curricula used in zoo and aquarium programs across the globe. Reading this book, I'm pleased to discover anew the passion, curiosity, and humorous sensibility that have always characterized Annette's work and her life. *Confessions of an Accidental Zoo Curator* is simply a delight.

Author's Note

It may seem startling that anyone can become a highly-respected specialist in a profession, much less a coveted one, by accident. Yet, as you'll soon discover, it happened to me. This is not the place to explain how it happened; the book will answer that query. Rather, it may be more interesting and better to explain why after stumbling into it, I became not only good at it, but also passionate about it.

In order to truly grasp the roots of this passion, one would need to understand the family I came from. My parents emerged from WWII exhausted survivors of those who strove to annihilate them. They escaped the Nazi onslaught in Poland in 1939, only to be captured and interned in Soviet gulags. The mission of the gulags was to modernize the vast underpopulated regions of the Soviet empire using slave labor. In essence, they used human beings as tools until every ounce of energy drained from their starved bodies. As gulag inmates, my parents performed tasks for which they were totally ill-suited: digging ditches and canals, felling ancient forests, and picking cotton—all with a minimum of tools and all in exchange for one pita bread a day; a sustenance decreased if the "norm" was not achieved. My parents were the lucky ones. They survived, but untold thousands died of starvation and disease. This was only a minor inconvenience for the Soviet government; there were plenty of others to take their place until they too would fall.

After amnesty was announced for Polish inmates, pursuant to an agreement between Joseph Stalin and the Polish government in exile, my parents journeyed south to the foothills of the Himalayas to shelter until the end of WWII. And this is where I was born. My earliest impressions of nature were the majestic snow-covered peaks of the Pamir mountains and the poppy fields that grew in the valley below.

My parents and I returned to Poland when they thought it was safe to embark on a 3,000-mile journey. Their arrival in a country that used to be home was not welcoming. Strangers occupied my parents' former homes, and everyone they had known and loved had been murdered.

As one might imagine, living with parents who survived such traumas was sometimes difficult for a child: they tended to be overprotective and spoke frequently of the lost loved ones. I knew my extended family only from stories. We had not one relative who could share our birthdays and holidays. We were the end of the line.

My parents did their level best to compensate for the losses, but having pets was not in the cards. We lived in a tiny two-room apartment in the center of one the country's most industrial cities. And to be perfectly honest, as individuals who grew up in orthodox Jewish homes, neither of my parents had much experience with pets, because keeping animals at home was somewhat anathema to orthodox Jews, unless they were carp for gefilte fish. So, my childhood was devoid not only of family, but also of pets—making me a most unlikely candidate for my eventual career.

When the opportunity to work at the world's premier zoological institution fell from the sky, I had no idea that, eventually, the notion of saving life would be exactly what I needed to heal my own sense of what it feels like to reach the end of family... the end of all possibilities. It actually didn't take too long for me to fall in love with all life forms, from lowly hermit crabs to magnificent gorillas, from boa constrictors to wolves.

There was so much affirmation of life, with its power to inspire and to refresh, that greeted me daily as I entered the exquisite Rainey gates to the Bronx Zoo: barking sea lions, hooting gibbons, even screaming peafowl making their daily forbidden rounds. These were the sounds of life and joy that took me so far away from my childhood, growing up in the shadow of the Holocaust. Now my mission was to do my small part to prevent the extinction of animal life. I threw myself into this mission with the zeal of one who possesses a visceral understanding of loss.

If you have decided to join me on a journey of discovery, I hope you'll experience it in the same wide-eyed, amazed manner I did, first as an enchanted novice, and later as a deeply engaged explorer of the animal world.

♦ ♦ ♦

I would like to thank the many individuals who made this book possible. First and foremost, I am indebted to my husband for encouraging me to share some of the stories that were the background music of our lives. I could not have worked to disseminate new strategies for wildlife education around the U.S. and the world without his steadfast support and mammoth contribution as a parent. My daughter's and son's insistence that we keep a variety of pets and their joy in my zoo job were surely factors in my heartfelt engagement with my career.

Professionally, I need to thank countless colleagues in the zoo universe—too many to name them all—who were open to new ideas and always eager to collaborate. Ann Robinson was the consummate professional whose talent in appealing to every kind of audience made her a superb trainer, an outstanding colleague and friend. Kathleen Lamattina is a woman I'd like to have been, a natural "animal person" who knows how to nurture any living creature. Her care of the teaching collection of animals at the Bronx Zoo is without peer.

I must single out two remarkable pioneer scientists who had the vision and imagination to consider educators as partners in saving wildlife. If it weren't for Dr. George Schaller and Dr. Alan Rabinowitz, our curricular programs might have never made their way to China and Belize and from there to so many other countries.

I am forever grateful to James Doherty, the world renowned General Curator of the Bronx Zoo, who reviewed this manuscript and offered suggestions. I also have a debt of gratitude to Lee Ehmke, Director & CEO of the Houston Zoo, whose creativity and vision in zoological designs has made revolutionary improvements to several zoos across the U.S. Finally, I owe my deep respect to the legendary conservationist and pioneer of modern zoo exhibition, former CEO of the Bronx Zoo William G. Conway, whose vision allowed me to play in an environment most conducive to creative education programs.

Note: Some names and identifying details have been changed to protect the privacy of individuals.

CHAPTER 1

Anetka and Her Pomeranian

My arrival in the industrial city of Lodz, Poland, after journeying from the foothills of the Himalayas just after the end of WWII, was a huge shock to my system. I was three years old. The weeks of traveling by cattle train, sleeping on the floor and being sponge-bathed with the water dripping off the locomotive had made me lose all sense of home. The day after we arrived, my mother gave birth to my brother in a homeless shelter for Jewish refugees. A short time later, a friend we had known before the war took all four of us to live with him and his wife in a tiny one-room apartment. The baby, sick with a serious infection, screamed around the clock. The place was so cramped we had to navigate carefully around the washbasin, coal bin, cots, and diaper pail. Worst of all, my parents were depressed after their return to their homeland to hear the horrific news that their immediate family members had all been exterminated.

It took two years for my parents to secure their own living quarters and find jobs. Things would have looked up for little Anetka, as I was called then, if I hadn't contracted a tuberculosis infection and been shipped off to a sanatorium a few hours away from home. Torn away from my family, I was miserable and couldn't wait to return home. But upon recovery, I was sent away again, this time to stay with distant relatives in Torun, a city more than one hundred miles northwest, until all risk to my baby brother had passed.

When I returned, my parents showered me with attention to the extent they could. They both worked long hours—my father as an administrator in a textile plant, and my mother in her tiny corset shop. To improve my mood, my mother bought a magnificent huge sleeping doll with long black hair and blue eyes that clicked whenever I laid her down to sleep. I don't really know why I didn't like this doll. Maybe it was her frozen expression or that unnatural sound when her eyes closed, but she frightened me and eventually my mother gave her away. There seemed little anyone could do to lift my spirits.

One day, my father returned from work with a big grin. "Mama is bringing you an amazing gift when she comes home," he said, lifting me up in the air and giving me an affectionate squeeze. I inhaled the starch of his shirt and felt instantly comforted.

"What is it, Daddy?" I jumped up and down as soon as he lowered me.

"I can't spoil the surprise," he said, winking.

I stood on my tiptoes near the window, trying to spot Mama coming home for what seemed like hours. I didn't even go to the bathroom and jumped on one foot, then the other, because I didn't want to miss her arrival. But eventually nature won over. While I was in the bathroom, I heard a strange sound. Was it a bark? No, it was too high-pitched for a dog. I hurried out and spotted Mama—she stood in her coat and hat in the middle of the living room, holding a bag and rocking it as if it were a baby. "What's in there?" I asked.

"I have something special for you, Anetka, but you must promise to take good care of it."

"What is it? What is it?"

I approached the bag and a small furry head popped out. "A puppy!" I exclaimed, then remembered something Mama had told me earlier. "But… but you said we couldn't have pets in the apartment."

"Well, I decided to make an exception," she said, smiling and setting the bag on the floor.

A fluffy white ball of fur emerged, its curious black eyes resembling the coal in our bin. It was shivering.

"It's cold in here," Mama said. "We have to light the stove. The poor thing is freezing."

"Maybe it's frightened to be in a new place," my father said as Mama lifted it into her arms and stroked its fur. I just stood there wide-eyed, a mixture of excitement and apprehension roiling in my stomach.

After the stove was lit and the room became warmer, the small creature began barking short high-pitched yips. This alarmed me, as did the tiny sharp teeth visible in its narrow muzzle. "Come closer, don't worry, Anetka," Mama said. "Sit next to me on the sofa and I'll show you something."

I advanced cautiously, intrigued, as Mama cuddled the puppy in her lap. I perched on the edge of the sofa, a safe distance away.

"Look," Mama said, dipping her hand into the bag that had held the dog.

"A brush for my braids?" I asked, confused.

Mama laughed. "No silly, it's for the puppy. I will teach you how to brush her fur."

"Will I have to touch her? Will she bite me?"

"She won't if you don't hurt her. You'll have to be gentle and brush her back, not her face. Just like I'm gentle when I brush your hair."

I wasn't sure I liked the sound of that. The puppy began to squirm and jumped off Mama's lap onto the floor, spinning around in circles, chasing her tail. Her small pointy ears pricked up. "Isn't she adorable?" Mama said.

"I've heard that Pomeranians are very active and lively," my father said.

"That's exactly the reason I got it for Anetka," Mama said.

"Is her name Panamanian?" I asked.

They both laughed. "No, no, she doesn't come from Panama. *Pomeranian* is the name of her breed. And in all this excitement we forgot to give you a chance to name her."

"Oh, we studied about Panama in school," I said, disappointed that my new knowledge of geography hadn't come in handy. I closed my eyes and tried to come up with a good name. "I know! I know! I have the best name: *Sniezka!*" I said proudly.

"What a good idea," Mama said, surveying the fluff ball. "She does look like a Snow White!"

After all the excitement, I went to bed cheerful, yet still somewhat uneasy, especially when I thought about how Mama had said I'd have to take care of Sniezka after school. I wasn't convinced I was up to the task. I had never even touched a real animal before. Sniezka's sharp little teeth looked like the needles that frightened me in the sanatorium, and I knew that Marysia, our nanny, wasn't fond of animals, so she might not help me. And I wasn't entirely sure I liked the way Mama cuddled Sniezka.

♦♦♦

I woke up so late the next morning that I hardly had a chance to think about Sniezka before I rushed off to school. In class, when the teacher asked us to read from our primer, all the pictures seemed to turn into Sniezka's toothy grin. Instead of counting the crayons in the math problems, I tried to remember how many teeth I saw in her muzzle.

When I returned from school, I heard Sniezka even before the door opened. She was barking furiously, trying to jump on me as soon as Marysia opened the door. I stepped back, terrified, not sure what to do.

"Anetka, I have to do some grocery shopping and then the laundry," Marysia announced, stepping back from the frantic puppy. "Be a good girl and do your homework while I'm gone. Sniezka will keep you company." With that she picked up the shopping bag and walked out, taking my little brother with her.

"Wait!" I shouted, but it was too late. I heard her bounding down the stairs.

I walked down the long, darkened corridor leading from the front door to the living room. Along the way, I passed the kitchen door, which was closed, because it was always cold in there unless Marysia had lit the cooking stove. The puppy followed me close behind. Its barking had subsided, but instead, a low growly sound—like a motor—came from her belly. Afraid that she would nip at my heels, I tried to keep a few steps ahead. I made it to the dining table, which was my usual place to do schoolwork. So far so good.

Keeping my eyes on the dog, I dumped the contents of my book bag on the table so I could do my first grade arithmetic. Suddenly, Sniezka began to bark furiously again and jumped up on my leg. With each bark, my fear grew into terror. In my mind, she was transformed into a giant creature. I thought of all the wolf stories I knew. The illustrations in my *Little Red Riding Hood* book came to mind and I clearly saw the drops of blood dripping from the wolf's open jaw. I was sure Sniezka was about to go for my face.

Maybe she's hungry, I thought, so I crept back toward the kitchen and opened the door. A blast of cold air hit my face as I entered. She followed me. I searched for the bowl of dog food Mama had told me about, but couldn't find it. Instead, I filled a bowl with water and set it on the floor. Sniezka approached, then lapped at it greedily. Maybe she was just thirsty. I felt relieved, but fearing she'd follow me and begin barking again and showing those flesh-piercing teeth, I snuck out and closed the door.

But as I started on my homework, the frantic high-pitched barking resumed. I didn't know what to do. Conflict raged in my heart. Should I let Sniezka out of the kitchen and take a chance she'd bite me, or let her stay there until Marysia returned? I decided to wait a while and to my delight, after I'd completed several pages of my math problems, the barking stopped. I felt calmer.

Marysia was away for so long on that day that Mama returned from work before her. She called for me and I opened the front door. Her cheeks were pink with the cold and looked lovely, set off by her dark hair. "I expected Sniezka to be with you," Mama said, unwrapping her scarf and pulling off her gloves. "Where is she?"

"Ah...she is um… in the kitchen."

"Why? It's freezing in there," Mama said with a frown on her face and immediately dashed to the kitchen.

I was nervous about having imprisoned Sniezka there, so I tiptoed back to the living room. A moment later Mama came into the room looking angrier than I had ever seen her. She was cradling the shivering Sniezka, who was now totally silent. "Look what you have done to this poor creature!" She yelled at me. "The cold could kill her."

She went into the bedroom and put Sniezka under her fluffy down quilt. "I'll try to warm her. I am so disappointed in you, Anetka. You have done a terrible thing."

"I… I… will do better next time," I stammered as tears sprang to my eyes.

"There won't be a next time. I'm taking her back in the morning." She said it so decisively I knew nothing would change her mind.

I was ashamed of locking up Sniezka and a little embarrassed too, because I was glad the beast with a million sharp teeth would be out of my life. That episode sealed my fate for a childhood without the companionship of a trusted animal friend. It would be nearly a decade before my next encounter of the wild kind.

Chapter 2

Bronx Natives

I should have been more careful with my friend Bully. I will always feel guilty about his sad fate, but in a strange way he later became an emblem of redemption for me, one that ultimately led to my career.

I was an urban dweller most of my life, up until my last year in high school. My family had left Poland for Israel with the great exodus of 1957. Two years later, we came to New York to seek a better life and settled in the Bronx. Here, as in Lodz and Tel Aviv, concrete and glass formed most of my vistas. I was as much a part of that rigid, unyielding habitat as the pigeons perching on the window ledges, the roaches roaming in the crevices of cupboards, and the mice rustling in the plaster walls of city buildings.

Then my family moved. It was a tiny shift in terms of distance, probably no more than a quarter mile, but meta-phorically speaking, it was transformational. As I began my first year of college, our new apartment was in a traditional high rise building, but it overlooked the immense verdant expanse of Van Cortlandt Park in Northwest Bronx.

What a thrill it was to look out the living room windows and see the park in all its glory, nearly 1,200 acres of woodland forests, marshes, meadows and fields. That was the moment I realized that for all the years before, my eyes and my soul had been deprived of green vistas. I had been a victim of the (as-of-yet unnamed) sickness: nature deficit disorder.

Humans have evolved from nature. For millennia, we were inextricably linked to the natural world in intimate ways. Our ancestors made cozy beds of leaves up in the canopies of trees and ate all manner of plants. But over time we began to lose, little by little, our connection to all things green, so that now most people are as comfy in their high urban apartments as their ancestors once were in trees. For too many city folks, especially those who can't afford vacations away from urban dwellings, the color green is more reminiscent of money than of nature.

One thing was certain: the landscape surrounding our new apartment would allow me to reconnect to what had been lost. At first I found it difficult to comprehend how such a lush oasis could exist in a borough better known for its slums and crime than for life forms that coexisted peacefully: oaks and hickory trees, sweet gum, bluebirds, barred owls, red-tailed hawks and wood ducks, cattails and fish, frogs and water lilies, snapping turtles and muskrats, and dragonflies buzzing along the shaded banks of the lakes.

It was the botany course in my first year at the City College of New York that got me out to explore the immense park outside my windows, not just with my eyes, but by walking through its meadows and trails, pausing to listen to the murmuring of its waters and admire the songs of the birds perched on its ancient trees.

Professor Copeland was an inspirational teacher and I plunged into his course like a frog into a pond, so to speak. He urged us to go beyond mere observations of the plants on our park field trips. "Don't just look for ferns, fungi and mosses, conifers and flowering plants. I want you to see, smell, photograph and record every living thing—with an extra dose of attention to all things green."

On one of my park hikes to catalogue the aquatic plants, I stumbled onto the bank of a large fresh water lake off the Putnam Trail. The broad-leaved cattails with their graceful shoots swayed gently in the May breeze. I had strayed away from my classmates and stopped, transfixed by the absence of city noise, to look at the crystalline droplets of water glistening on the water lilies.

Suddenly, I heard a strange, unfamiliar noise—like a mechanical tool scraping. What could that be? My city ears, used to cars honking and police sirens, did not recognize the sound. Then I heard it again, a deep "jug—o—rum" at short intervals.

After a few minutes, the rest of my class reached my corner of this urban paradise, and a classmate pointed to a stone-like greenish blob at the edge of the lake. "Oh, look at that bullfrog," he said.

"What could that sound it's making mean?" I asked of no one in particular.

"It's breeding season. Must be plenty of bullfrog tadpoles around," someone speculated.

I bent down to look more closely at the brackish water and dipped my clean pickle jar in it to see what would come up. Almost immediately I scooped up what looked like a bizarre fish. It was a dark greenish-gray, with black spots and a long undulating tail. It swam in graceful circles, to avoid bumping into the glass.

"Whoa, you got yourself a huge bullfrog tadpole," my classmate said.

I was about to dump it back into the water when something made me look at the critter again. He was such a lively fellow! In an absurd moment of fantasy, it occurred to me that if I took him home and watched him grow, eventually he'd turn into a beautiful frog prince! So, on a lark, I decided to bring him to my family's apartment.

Had I given it any real thought, I'd have quickly realized my parents would not look kindly on having this amphibian in their home. Pet keeping was not a tradition in our family, afflicted as it was by nature deficit disorder. So, I wasn't about to reveal that I had lugged this slimy critter home to live with us. I decided that Bully—I had named him immediately—would be a fugitive, living in a jar under my bed. I'd observe his changes and record them dutifully, as Dr. Copeland had suggested. Bully wasn't a plant, but he would be as green as a lily pad when he completed his mysterious metamorphosis.

Keeping Bully happy and healthy required research and surreptitiously changing his water and cleaning his jar in the bathroom. I didn't dare to use the kitchen sink, lest he be discovered. Since our apartment had only one bathroom, I'd get chastised regularly. "What are you doing in there so long? I need to use the bathroom," one of my parents would call out in frustration.

"I'll be right out. I have a stomach ache," I'd reply. Then my mother would want to make me chamomile tea, so I had to become more creative with my diversions. "I'm shaving my legs. I'm tweezing my eyebrows. I'm painting my nails. I'm having trouble with the faucet. I'm inhaling steam for my cough." I knew that eventually I'd run out of explanations, so I contorted my schedule to care for Bully when my parents were out of the house.

Months passed and although Bully changed a little, he was nowhere near his adult bullfrog self. How long would this take? I went to the library to do some research, and found that it could be two to three years! I had no idea bullfrogs took so long to mature. Maybe that's why they are so long-lived, seven to nine years on the average. At this rate, Bully would still be with me when I graduated from college and graduate school, maybe even when I got married! I could show my wedding guests how my new husband looked before he was transformed into a prince.

I didn't know how long my charade could go on, unnoticed. But on days when I was in a bad mood or nervous about an upcoming exam, I'd pull the jar out from beneath my bed and watch Bully. The wave-like motion of his delicate undulating tail made me calmer, and each time I decided he was worth the trouble.

Of the more than twenty thousand eggs his mother had laid, he was the lucky fellow to move into my bedroom. We were companions of sorts, bonding across the huge divide between our species. I was perfectly aware that Bully didn't get much out of our relationship, if one could characterize it as such, but I knew we had one thing in common: we had both originally emerged from water.

◆◆◆

Dr. Copeland's class ended and I was grateful to have been inspired by him to observe nature in all its marvelous manifestations. Each new fact I uncovered in my research exploded in my brain like fireworks. Who knew that flower petals had an invisible pattern of lines guiding insects to their nectar? Or that *Rafflesia*, the corpse flower, smells like rotten meat so it can attract flies for pollination? Or that Giant Sequoias can live to be 5,000 years old? The world of plants and the animals that depend on them took powerful hold of my imagination.

By late fall of the following semester, Bully was still in his infancy. One day I was in a hurry as I was cleaning his jar. Normally I'd invert it to decant the dirty water through the holes I'd made on the metal screw-top. This time I was distracted and tilted the jar over the toilet bowl with the top off. Bully fell into the toilet and immediately swam down the drain!

I stood there, horrified. My pet of all those months was gone—and to such an awful fate! Would he meet the legendary alligators in the New York sewers? Would the effluent kill him instantly? Would he suffer? Or maybe I was all wrong. Maybe he was delighted to be freed from the glass jar that had been his prison all these months. I had no idea. I knew only one thing: from then on, I'd be nervous sitting on the toilet, lest Bully in his frog prince incarnation come for revenge.

After all, I'd learned that adult bullfrogs are aggressive—and carnivorous.

CHAPTER 3

A Horse of Another Color

The joyous laughter of children scampering off the play-ground slide suddenly turned into ear-piercing shrieks as three toddlers began to struggle over a tricycle. I had spent the better part of the summer in this playground with my children. Now, as I strained to hear the conversation with another mother, I realized that the place was starting to get on my nerves. I shifted my gaze to the sidewalk just outside the park and noticed a woman in heels and an elegant business suit with a leather briefcase dangling from one hand and a young boy's hand in the other. She must be coming from work and has just picked up her child, I observed. How I envied her. Guiltily, right then and there, I firmed up a decision to return to work full-time. My youngest child was nearly four, after all, and I had been vacillating for months. As much as I loved watching my children grow and learn, the allure of adult conversation and a challenge greater than picking up toys from the floor and reading the same story for the umpteenth time was irresistible.

Before my children were born I worked in a sterile laboratory doing cancer research at the renowned Sloan Kettering Cancer Institute in New York. I don't mean sterile in the sense of being spare and modern; it was sterile in the biological sense, a lab irradiated so that no contaminants would come in contact with the samples being studied. I sat all day, attired in a lab coat and rubber gloves, isolated in a glass cubicle. My only contact with people was in passing, coming in and out of the isolation room, or meeting with my boss to discuss the work.

The goal of the research was noble, but the day-to-day routine of sitting alone, surrounded by petri dishes growing different cancer cell lines, was much less glamorous than it sounded when I told friends I was a cancer researcher. This job was ideal for a true introvert, not someone like me who enjoyed interacting with people. And I knew that when I returned to work, I'd want to engage with living breathing human beings rather than just their cells.

For a time after I left the lab, when my children were still very young, I worked part-time as a teacher, but it was not something I enjoyed as much as I thought I would. Substitute teachers rarely get assigned the same school, much less the same class of children. Sometimes the work felt more like babysitting, despite my ardent desire to transmit important concepts to the students. No matter what I did, or how hard I worked to prepare engaging lessons, I always remained *the sub*, a specie that's adept at ducking spitballs.

One day, while riding the subway, my eye caught an ad: faces of smiling people declaring, "I got my job through the *New York Times.*" Surprisingly, they included executives and other professionals, not just the secretaries and cooks I had seen advertised in the paper. When I got home, I decided to scour the want ads in *The Times* more diligently, and within a week, I had sent out several resumes, despite the lingering pinpricks of doubt at the back of my mind. Were the children ready to be left with a babysitter? Where would I find a qualified person to care for them? I decided that no matter what, I'd only accept an offer close to home, so I could be available quickly in case of any emergency.

One of the ads was especially enticing and had an aura of mystery about it. It solicited applicants interested in coordinating volunteers at a Bronx cultural institution. They didn't specify which one, which made me even more curious. I searched my mind—were there even *any* major cultural institutions in our borough? Perhaps it was a library or a historical society. I tossed my resume in the mailbox and nearly forgot about it.

A few days later, the phone rang, loud and insistent, waking my children from a nap. "Who is calling?" I asked the woman on the line.

"The Bronx Zoo," she said.

"THE BRONX ZOO?" I yelled out. "Why are you calling me?" Thinking it was a silly prank, I nearly hung up.

"I have your resume in front of me," the woman said, and checked my last name.

"Umm... " I didn't know what to say, but the caller rescued me.

"We are the Bronx cultural institution you responded to. We don't list our name to discourage unsuitable applicants. Sometimes we get real animal nuts trying to work here."

"Oh, of course, that makes sense," I said, wondering what made them think I was a zoo person. Maybe it's my scientific background and training, I concluded tentatively, and we set up an interview appointment.

◆◆◆

It had been ten years since my last close encounter of the animal kind. Bully, my pet bullfrog tadpole, swam into my mind's eye. The notion of working in a zoo, a real zoo, and a world-class zoo at that, seemed funny. I couldn't picture myself getting as close to an elephant as I did back in Poland when I was five, just so my Dad could take a picture. The hulking beast had towered over me as I stood there trying not to pee in my pants and hoping it wouldn't step on my new Mary Janes. And yet the idea exerted a strong pull. I had always been fascinated with living creatures, and zoology and botany classes had always been my favorite. The Bronx Zoo had a sterling reputation and it was close to home. *Whoa!* I stopped myself. I hadn't even had the interview.

Since I had never in my wildest dreams imagined myself working at a zoo, I had no idea how to dress for the interview. Was this the kind of place where employees dressed in uniforms? I couldn't picture anyone there dressed in a suit and tie. And what about the women? How did they dress for work? Boots or high-heeled shoes? Dresses or pants? I had no clue and decided to take the middle road. I slipped into my favorite blue-green mini-dress, quite in fashion at the time. My reasoning went something like this: these are the colors of nature, and if I feel comfortable, I will be more relaxed.

I brushed my long hair to a shine and pulled on black high-heeled boots. A long honey colored sheepskin coat with large gold buckles completed the look. I looked at the mirror. Did I look too bohemian? Too sexy? Nerves muddled my judgment. But my husband gave me a wink and a thumbs-up, and I was good to go.

I arrived at the interview filled with adrenaline and trepidation. My heels clicked on the stone steps of the Administration building. Not the right sound for this place, I thought. And what if someone asked me animal questions? I hadn't cracked a zoology text in a decade. It would be bad enough to be rejected, but far worse to be made a fool. I soon found out my interviewer would be a world-famous reptile expert, a mover and shaker in the international wildlife conservation community. At that moment, reptile biology seemed farther away than New Jersey.

Dr. W. had a penetrating gaze and a cool handshake. He stood up straight, and though he was not old, his well-trimmed reddish beard gave him the look of someone belonging to the previous century, a specimen from the period when the zoo was new. His office, ensconced in an 1899 Beaux Arts building, was steeped in history. I was immediately struck by the imposing floor-to-ceiling mahogany bookcases filled with weighty leather-bound volumes, no doubt filled with reptile minutia and obscure scientific facts known only to experts. I cringed. What could he possibly ask me?

But he didn't ask anything just yet; he simply clarified that public education was not exactly his area, but—and here I had the impression he'd sigh if it was appropriate—he was handling it for the moment.

Then he picked up my resume, squinted at it, and tossed it back on the desk, re-directing his gaze on me. "How many children do you have?" he asked.

I was taken aback by this question, and for a brief instant thought this may be a family friendly work place—not quite, I soon found out.

"So, do you plan on having any more," he asked, after I replied to the first question.

"Ah… well… what do you mean?" I was nonplussed. I understood the words, but not the intent behind them.

"Well, the world is overpopulated. If people continue breeding like rabbits, there will be no room for wildlife," he announced with, well, was that a *sneer*? I couldn't tell for sure.

I swallowed hard and felt my cheeks begin to glow red. I was embarrassed, having never discussed my child-bearing plans with anyone but my husband. And I was getting more than a little irritated by this line of questioning. My womb was not his business!

"I'm not sure I can answer. I don't know yet," I tried for something semi-conciliatory, though I really wanted to tell him to buzz off. I stared at him and noticed a tiny pin on his lapel. In an instant, I figured it out: it was a vasectomy pin. Not like the boisterous vasectomy buttons of today, his was a discrete, incomplete gold circle with a tiny arrow at one end. So this man either didn't want any children, or he had had enough. His stance on population control was as clear as the small mountain streams he wanted to protect from human intrusion for the benefit of vipers.

"I hope you won't be like some of the Irish who work here: seven kids at a minimum," he commented after a long pause.

I could hardly believe my ears. He was interrogating me on a private matter that was irrelevant to the interview. Or maybe birth control *was* a requirement for this job. Would I be forced to get my tubes tied? Give my children up for adoption? Picket against Irish Catholics? I could think of any number of responses, but each of them would disqualify me immediately, so I kept quiet.

Perhaps it was the astonished look on my face—I could barely keep my mouth from hanging open—but Dr. W. managed a wan smile and stood up. I thought the interview was finished, but saw him approach the book-laden shelves and reach for a thick tome.

I froze. As uncomfortable as his previous questions made me, now I'd be quizzed on reptilian biology. Ugh, it's just about over, I thought.

He sat back down and thumbed through the book while I attempted to come up with an excuse about my rusty zoology. "Here it is!" He smiled. "Take a look." He pushed the open volume toward me and a knot formed in my stomach. What I didn't know about reptiles could easily fill a volume. I picked up the book and saw a beautiful photo of a stocky horse with an erect mane. An immediate sense of relief washed over me—a mammal!

"How do you pronounce its name? he asked.

I relaxed. "This is a *Przewalski* horse," I said. Not only did I recognize it, but its name was printed right below the photo and for me, a Polish speaker, it was a snap to pronounce the odd "*rz*" combination: tongue gymnastics required.

"You have no idea how long I've wondered about the correct pronunciation of this name!" Dr. W. exclaimed. His tone turned reverent.

"These animals are all but extinct in the wild, you must know that."

"Yes, I know. They are Mongolian wild horses, native to Asia, near my place of birth." I was glad to volunteer this bit of knowledge, but hoped he wouldn't ask me how they acquired this name. I had no idea.

"You were not born here?" Now it was his turn to be surprised.

"I was born in Kyrgyzstan and came to the U.S. when I was sixteen."

He whistled. "But your English…it's so American."

"I'm a quick learner," I said, sensing the interview tilting my way.

The meeting did not last much longer. He shook my hand and said I'd be hearing from the Society soon. Society? It took me a moment to figure out what he meant.

In its early days, the zoo was known as the New York Zoological Park. Later, the public gave it the much-beloved nickname The Bronx Zoo. However, at its founding in 1895, the actual name was the New York Zoological Society. Given the number of New York glitterati supporting this private not-for-profit institution, "the Society" was, indeed, the most apt description.

♦♦♦

Two days later I received a call that the job was mine if I still wanted it. A mixture of excitement and apprehension flooded my mind. I had a job offer in a prestigious scientific institution and it was close to home. It met all my criteria. But was I up to this job? The discussion with my husband went into the night.

"You can do it, Annette." David was enthusiastic. "You love learning new things."

"But what if I have to work late and I still want to continue with my graduate work?" I agonized.

"Don't be such a worry wart, I can make supper too." David did his best to calm me. After hours of debate and a sleepless night I had the answer: yes. I knew the job would challenge me intellectually, but I had no idea how much.

Sometimes, it's better not to know.

CHAPTER 4

Heads and Horns

I stood before the mirror, dressed in a stylish green silk dress, with pumps to match and a jade necklace. "Is this what a zoo employee looks like?" I asked the mirror. I had no idea, since I had never imagined doing this type of work. The fresh memory of a juicy desk job offer at Con Edison the week after I had accepted the zoo position buzzed in my head. But I had rejected it for something more exciting, I reminded myself: animals.

As a student, they'd always fascinated me: their behaviors, ingenious adaptations for survival, habitats, and life in the wild. I devoured the information in my zoology classes, wrote papers, conducted research, read books, even watched them in the wild—but close physical contact was never an option. Growing up in small city apartments, I had never had pets—except for Bully, and does he even count?—and after my experience with Sniezka, I had never developed a craving to cuddle a puppy or to snuggle with a kitten.

Despite Dr. W.'s views on children, I accepted the zoo's job offer *because* of my children: it was close to my home. With two under the age of six, I didn't want to schlep into Manhattan and be a subway ride away in case of an emergency. The zoo was just a fifteen- minute drive, even in bad traffic. And from a professional perspective, what could be better than working in the most highly-regarded zoo in the world? This job would challenge me and engage me in the kind of material I had loved as a student. Best of all, telling my children Mommy was going to the zoo made them squeal with delight, especially when I assured them they'd be able to visit often.

I scurried around the apartment, nervously glancing at the clock as I tied up loose ends, looking for a misplaced box of crayons and Jeremy's lost sock. As I applied my makeup, all I could think of was those darn missing crayons. I searched under the sofa, in the kitchen drawers, and rummaged through the overstuffed toy box. I tried to hurry as I made Jessica's lunch, but I knew I couldn't skip making the moat in the peanut butter so the jelly wouldn't squish out and labeling the paper bag on *both* sides. It had been at least two years since I headed out to work so early. Now I had to make sure Jessica was ready for her first grade class, and that Jeremy's new babysitter was aware of his morning routine—farina and fruit for breakfast, playtime, story time with *Clifford the Red Dog*, then a nap with his favorite blanket.

That November day, I sped up on Moshulu Parkway—a green oasis, belying the decay and abandoned, rubble-strewn lots in much of the borough—weaving in and out of traffic. I wanted to get to my new office early to prepare mentally for the unknown. A man crossing Fordham Road reminded me of my strange job interview; he looked a lot like the head honcho who had made the decision to hire me. After my talk with Dr. W., I was fully aware of the Zoological Society's scope and illustrious history, but he had actually revealed very little about the position I'd occupy. All I knew was that it was in the Education Department and that it would involve coordinating volunteers and possibly some teaching. I had two years of teaching experience under my belt and had coordinated volunteers in our food coop. That's why the job had sounded simple and clear at the interview, and I hadn't wanted to ask too many questions. In any case, there were hints that the department lacked leadership, something I had tucked deep in my brain, filed away for reference. "Could I lead this education unit at some future time?" I had asked myself, but my logical mind shot the idea down before it could bloom. The interviewer was several levels removed from the day-to-day management of the department, and he would probably not have had many answers for me anyway.

Entering the zoo via the monumental bronze Rainey Memorial Gate, I tried to take it all in. The gate's magnificently sculpted menagerie exuded a dignified elegance, and I stopped to look at it. Three bears were under the left arch, three antelopes under the right, and a lion was perched high above them on top of a central tree, surveying all. A baboon and a lioness were crouching on the sides, and three tortoises were supporting the entire grouping. Impressive! Entry through this gate seemed like a good omen.

I parked in the circular lot next to a beautiful three-tiered marble fountain and clambered out of the car, trying not to scuff my new shoes. At first, the fountain's baroque whimsical sea creatures seemed out of place in this impoverished section of the Bronx, but as I glanced behind me back at the gate, I saw that they were all of a piece, evoking the rich history of this *grand dame* of New York's cultural institutions. I felt glad to be here instead of stuck in a sterile lab or roaming the corporate corridors of Con Edison.

"Too much sightseeing," I admonished myself and turned toward the imposing, wide staircase leading to the central court. I saw several employees in brown uniforms and sturdy work boots going up, then glanced at my high heels and wondered if I would look like an amateur or even a joke to my colleagues, whoever they were. On my way up, I passed stone sculptures of jaguars crouching on pedestals, ready to sprint. The place had an air of grandeur I hadn't noticed when I came for the interview. The jaguars, though inert, gave me a shiver. Would I ever be asked to handle something as fierce? Nah, I'll just counsel volunteers or stand in front a class and lecture. Right?

Before I entered the one-story building where my office would be, I stopped and read the inscription on its pale brick and cement façade: National Collection of Heads and Horns. A passing bit of levity lightened my nervousness. This is where the educators live! Is this the "heads" reference? And the horns? Are those the obstinate students they are trying to instruct?

The glass doors on the ground floor were closed, so I wandered downstairs to the basement level. An attractive young woman sat behind the desk, filing her nails. "You the new instructor?" she asked, raising her neat black eyebrows, studying me.

"Yes. Excuse me, are you in charge here?"

She laughed, a high-pitched titter. "I wish… "

"So, who'll tell me what to do?"

"No one really. We all know what we have to do."

And what would that be, I wanted to inquire, but felt it would mark me as a rookie forever. She studied me, focusing on my shoes—was it judgment, pity, or simply appreciation for my fashion sense, I wondered, feeling self-conscious.

Then she stood up and shook my hand, "I'm Evelyn," she said, smoothing her tight skirt. "Let me show you to your desk," she offered, walking me into the bowels of the lower level, pointing out the auditorium where classes were held, as well as the audio-visual studio and the conference room. She stopped at a desk under a window that faced outside. "Best real estate. You're facing the elk exhibit."

"Thank you," I said and settled in, looking at the animal books on the shelf near the desk and the bird posters on the wall.

"Oh, by the way, there are no classes scheduled today," she said, and returned to her desk where I imagined she would continue her manicure.

I didn't want to ask what instructors do on days with no classes, and decided to peruse the *Mammals of the World* reference book as a refresher course. I was glad to have time to settle into my office, but thought that if I were in charge there would be no such wasted idle time. Manicures on the job! Sheesh!

I craned my neck looking out the window trying to spot the elk, but they must have been in another area of the large enclosure—a chain-link fence surrounded the natural deciduous northeastern forest—because I could not find them.

Before I had a chance to reach for the book, a stocky woman in her late twenties, with shoulder-length brown hair and thick bangs, barged in to the office area. She wore a keeper's beige uniform and tall black rubber boots, and there was a no-nonsense air to her. Evelyn was right behind her, waving her hands in the air to dry the polish. "This is Kim. You need to go with her." Kim gave me a narrow-eyed a look as if I were an Andorean from *Star Trek*. Her lips seemed to turn down in disapproval. It must be my imagination, I thought.

"Let's go," she said abruptly. It sounded like an order.

"Where to?"

At first she didn't reply, and I grabbed my coat, which prompted another look of disdain. She didn't even have a jacket on. Hardy, these zoo folk, I thought. Could I become one of them?

"You'll see soon enough," she offered as we ascended the stairs and walked out into a gust of fall air sweeping leaves across the court. Seeing that she was not in a chatty mood, I followed her in silence. Soon we approached what I knew from visits with my kids to be the Children's Zoo. "Isn't this closed for the winter season?" I asked, surprised she was opening the gate.

"Yes, but this is where we keep the animals," she replied, her tone all business.

What animals might these be? I wondered. My most recent visit with the children came to mind. Chickens? Rabbits? Piglets? Kim led me to a small low building in the center of the Children's Zoo, inconspicuous because it stood behind a gray stockade fence. I had no idea why she was taking me there, but I was curious to see. The door opened and a gust of steam hit my face. I backed up and began unbuttoning my coat. A strong odor of fermenting fruit mixed with an unidentifiable musky scent reached my nostrils. Ugh! I tried to breathe through my mouth. Where was I? "We have to keep it warm for the reptiles," Kim said. "This place is so drafty it loses heat quickly."

All I could think was, reptiles? Reptiles? I hadn't seen any reptiles on my visit to the Children's Zoo. Were they in here?

The room was extremely cramped. Rows of stainless steel cages stacked high, nearly to the ceiling, stood along narrow aisles. Two keepers busied themselves chopping carrots, kale, and apples, weighing and measuring an assortment of pellets and other edibles I couldn't name. A cacophony of animal noises filled the small space: birds chirping, screeching, and scratching, various mewls I couldn't identify, growls, hisses, and an odd snoring sound. A washing machine whirred and a dryer produced rhythmic pings. One of the keepers looked up at me and said, "We do the wash in the morning." What could they be washing here, animal clothes? The place was a weird combination of Chinese laundry, diner, and a side show. What was I doing here? I walked past cages with hawks, ferrets, armadillos, owls, and an anteater. The strong animal stench that suffused the air made it unpleasant to breathe.

When an ear-piercing shriek came from behind me, Kim said, "Don't mind him. It's Romaine, our cockatoo. He does that sometimes." She then disappeared into one of the aisles. I turned to look at Romaine, a magnificent sulfur-crested bird with snowy white plumage. I moved closer to his cage to make space for the keeper who had appeared behind me and was cleaning out cages and delivering breakfast. A moment later Kim tapped my shoulder, and I turned around quickly.

"Here, hold it for a minute," she said. It took me a second to realize she was about to plop an enormous snake in my arms! I blanched. All my blood drained to my toes. The only animal I had ever held was my old pal Bully, the bullfrog, and he was always inside a glass jar! I saw the look in her eyes, and in a flash of awareness, I knew I was being tested. If I had no guts to hold this reptile, I might be out of a job on day one.

In a spasm of inner terror, I extended my arms. She placed the serpent on them. I prayed that my trembling knees would not give out. It was heavy, certainly heavier than the turkey I had bought at the grocery store just a few days before. In a flash, I decided: it's a male. And this boy was a good six feet long, its diameter so thick I couldn't close my fingers around him. At first I shifted him uncomfortably in my arms, while he made himself comfy, wrapping his fleshy tail around my waist. I felt his muscles contracting against the back of my silk dress and a reflexive shiver shot down my spine. I knew boas were constrictors who kill by squeezing their prey so that their lungs can't expand.

Kim said, "I should have told you, we use these animals in classes."

"We use this snake?" I asked, trying to sound casual as he began slithering toward my shoulder. Though I had never been this close to such a scaly creature, with its narrow head and unblinking eyes, I knew all about the anatomy of its jaw and teeth. Would he sink his backward-pointing needle-like choppers into my cheek? I wanted a job, but not this badly!

"This boa is getting too big. We won't use him much longer. He scares the little kids… and some teachers too," Kim added with a chuckle. I stood there, rigid and terrified, now hoping that if I remained very still the snake would mistake me for a tree. With each of Kim's comments the snake was getting closer and closer to my face. I contorted my neck to avoid his row of endless teeth.

"OK, I'm done with his cage," the other keeper turned back to me and lifted the squirming boa out of my sweaty hands. I let out the breath I'd been holding and realized that, unlike my hands, the boa's skin was perfectly dry and smooth.

"You have animal handling experience? Right?" Kim asked, belatedly.

"Well, sort of," I mumbled under my breath, thinking: well, I do now.

"Good, you'll need it. These animals are our teaching tools," Kim said with what seemed like a smug smile. "Well, now you know where to come get them before each class," and it was clear I had been dismissed. She must be mistaken, I thought. My job is to work with volunteers, not animals. Still, I felt glad to know where my department kept its "tools."

I glanced over at a shallow basin that looked like a bird bath on a low stand. In it, four foot-long black-streaked alligator hatchlings were pushing each other, lifting their narrow snouts, which were kept shut with rubber bands. These guys could grow to be 12-footers. What had I gotten myself into? Maybe I should have taken the Con Ed job after all, I thought.

"Ready for breakfast, buddy?" said the second keeper, as she tossed a freshly-killed rat into the boa's cage. Gulp.

I turned to leave and made my way out among the animal cases and bags of birdseed. "Keep in mind," Kim called out, pointing to the alligators, "Heels may not be the ideal footgear when wrestling these guys."

Alligator wrestling—surely beyond my job description!

I walked back to my office through the quiet of the central court, unable to shake the impression of the boa's rippling muscles and its slit-like, unblinking eyes. I hurried downstairs and sat at my new desk, trying to sort out my conflicting emotions. Evelyn was nowhere to be seen. A rustling of leaves outside caused me to turn toward my window. A magnificent male elk stood nearly eye-to-eye with me, a few feet away. His resplendent rack of antlers, a crown, was as regal as his stance. He surveyed the area, moving his head slowly, and just for one electric instant I thought our gaze met.

CHAPTER 5

Kid Gloves

One of my fellow instructors was Rob, a brawny young man with bulging biceps. He was wearing a T-shirt on this frigid fall day that showed off a Mr. America physique, and bragging to me about his personal collection of boas and pythons and how he needed to get some fresh rats to feed them. "You've handled animals, before, right?" he confirmed.

I swallowed hard and smiled. His super white teeth flashed me a smile in return.

"Great," he said, taking my lack of response as a "yes." "I'm glad you're not like some of those volunteers. They're all gung-ho to hold a critter, but they don't have the first idea about how to do it."

"So, what animals will we be using?" I asked, trying to sound nonchalant.

"Raptors," he said. "Next week we start the birds-of-prey series."

"Do you have any tame ones to show in class?" I asked.

"Well, I wouldn't call any of them tame—they're wild, after all. But some are more used to handling than others. The new ones get pretty spooked, especially birds like Harry."

"Who is he?"

"Harris Hawk," he said. "You'll probably be using him, but beware of those talons." He stretched out his arm and showed me deep, red gouges on the inside of his wrist.

I didn't know what to say. Gripped with terror, I only managed an incoherent, "Hmm . . ." He must have noticed, because he said, "I'll get you a leather glove, but I don't use one. Gloves are for wimps."

"You aren't calling me a wimp?" I laughed, secretly wishing once again that I had accepted that cushy Con Edison desk job.

"Nah, you're a newbie. Besides, you'll have the barred owl, the screech owl and the sparrow hawk to bring along with Harry."

Oh, God, two owls and two hawks! Why did they need doubles of everything?

◆◆◆

Zoo workers, I'd quickly come to realize, treat their work as if it were a sport: competition, dare-devil feats, and intense pride are the order of the day for these folks. How did I find myself among them? By a quirk of fate. And I supposed I could be competitive too… under the right circumstances.

When I first accepted the job, it was described as a position to coordinate the volunteers who flocked to the zoo because they cared about animals, but who secretly hoped for a chance to cuddle baby tigers or monkeys, or anything exotic. They were donating their time, so they had to be handled with care and courtesy, but their dreams of lion nuzzling and cheetah hugging had to be tamed. Yes, I thought, I can do that.

But between the job offer, which elicited howls of laughter from my neighbor Donna, who knew my discomfort with her cat and two Great Danes, and my first week at work, something had changed. I didn't learn until years later that there was an ongoing turf battle over the management of volunteers, since there were some very wealthy donors among them. When I arrived at the zoo, naïve and innocent, I thought I'd be drill sergeant to the volunteers, but I discovered shortly after my snake encounter that my job would primarily involve teaching the groups of school children who swelled the ranks of visitors each spring. Kids? More like a bunch of rowdies from what I had seen on my spring zoo visits with my children. I was not exactly pleased with the sudden job change, but I was growing to love the park, especially when it was quiet, like on the November day I started. I'd make the best of it. Little did I know that I would not only be teaching *about* animals, something I would be perfectly comfortable and competent doing, but that I'd actually be teaching *with* those real animals, not in books or exhibits, but in my own arms!

The following week, brawny Rob was out of the office, but he kept his promise. On Monday morning a black leather glove with a small note sat on my desk. All it said was "Good luck." Somehow, the single glove seemed almost menacing and it only increased my anxiety. But since I had little choice, I took the glove to the Children's Zoo animal holding facility so I could practice handling the birds. The discomfort in my stomach grew as the distance to the building shrank. Becoming comfortable handling the raptors, even without the glove by the time Rob returned, now became my goal. I'd show Rob I wasn't a sissy.

Best to start small, I thought, and so I began with the screech owl. It was one-third the size of the barred owl. I looked closely into its yellow eyes, trying to mesmerize it like a magician. It stared back at me, perhaps considering: friend or foe? I put on my glove and slowly stuck my fist into its cage. The owl made a strange bark-like noise and backed away. I wondered if the sight of the glove had frightened it. I moved my arm all the way into the cage slowly and murmured softly to the bird. It put its foot on my hand and gripped my gloved fingers tightly. I felt lucky it hadn't chosen to sit further up my arm. Although I was wearing a long-sleeved shirt, I knew the talons would puncture it. Have I ever had a tetanus shot? What a time to think of it!

Next I practiced with Barney, the barred owl. I knew how beneficial owls were in the ecosystem, how exquisitely adapted they are for their work, but my brain and my gut were out of sync. Barney's penetrating gaze and indignant attitude alarmed me. He stood at least two feet tall and had an imperious demeanor. He looked at me with what I took for disdain. I knew I'd admire him in the wild if I ever did spot such a secretive animal, but I'd not dare to get very close. Now I had to beguile him enough to get him to sit on my arm. What had I gotten myself into? Inwardly, I blessed Rob for the glove, because I'd never have thought of it on my own.

I figured the noises I had made to the screech owl worked well enough as owl language, so I tried them again. Barney looked interested. His dark brown, nearly black eyes, so different from other owls, were two deep pools. I stuck my arm in, causing him to hop off his perch and extend his impressive wings four feet across, then flap them soundlessly. Holy Moly—what if I take him out and he flies off my arm in class? I pictured a stampede of kids, running away screaming.

I took a deep breath and noticed a piece of leather hanging off his foot. That must be the jess I had read about, I thought, I'll need to grasp it to keep him from flying away. A momentary regret made me feel guilty that I wouldn't be able to let him fly. But first things first: I had to persuade this big guy to hop onto my arm. Finally, he took one cautious step toward me, lifting his taloned foot. I was amazed at how light he felt on my arm for his size, even lighter than the small Cornish hens I had taken out of the freezer that morning to cook for dinner.

Emboldened, I repeated the procedure with the sparrow hawk, who for his diminutive size squawked far louder than anyone would expect, though in the end he too stepped onto my gloved hand, and I held his jess tight as he seemed ready to take off at any minute. Harry was last, and true to Rob's description, the feistiest. Luckily he, like Barney, was kept in a very large cage, wide enough for him to spread his equally impressive dark chestnut wings. He sported a wary and aloof gaze in his hyper-focusing black eyes, offset by the yellow patches of skin below them. He followed my every move as only a vigilant spy could. Small wonder he was such an outstanding hunter, capable of spotting a rabbit a mile away. For now, I could only imagine his elegant aerial maneuvers. Being born not far from the Asian steppes, a land of legendary falconers, I tried to imagine myself there, standing under a brilliant blue sky, watching Harry soar on the thermals, eyeing marmots or polecats. The image calmed my nerves.

After several minutes of showing off, displaying his wings and casting his all-encompassing gaze in my direction, Harry decided to grace me by settling on my arm. I couldn't take my eyes off his lethal-looking razor-sharp, curved black talons. It was easy to see why Rob's arm was so gouged. Would I ever dare to handle Harry gloveless? It was impossible to imagine, but I hated the idea that Rob and the others would consider me a wimp. Even "newbie" was unflattering.

In the days that followed, I practiced with all the raptors, but especially Harry. I can't say that he recognized me, but each day he seemed more approachable and came toward me without so much posturing. I knew that hawks like him were more social than others, and his behavior toward me seemed proof positive. He did scratch my arm, though. Nothing lethal, but my husband laughed hard when he saw me dabbing anti-bacterial cream on my injuries. "Isn't your job exciting? he chuckled. "Soon you'll be taming lions."

"Oh, shut up, "I said, bearing my battle scars proudly.

Rob was back in time for my first raptor class the next Monday. "Listen," he said, "I'll teach you a great trick that'll wow the kids."

What now? Rob was such a daredevil. Who knew what crazy idea he had? "See this long tube?" He held out a four-foot gray cardboard tube that must have held a poster once.

"What's it for?" I asked.

"When you stand at the front of the auditorium demonstrating Harry, let go of the jess when I give you the signal. I'll stand in the back of the room holding this tube."

"I don't get it. Why?"

"You see, Harry is a hunter. He'll think the tube is a snake and will shoot across the room over the kids heads and attack the tube."

I was nonplussed. "Really?"

♦♦♦

I read widely about the ecology and behavior of diurnal and nocturnal raptors, and couldn't wait to share what I had learned. When I finally got to the classroom, audible gasps filled the room when I told the children how true falcons, like the merlin, have a special tooth they use to break their prey's neck; how some kites can snatch a whole baby rabbit; how eagles fish with their feet; and how some vultures open eggs by throwing stones at them. When I was finished discussing raptors, I asked the students to remain perfectly still and to not be afraid. "You're about to get an idea of how hawks hunt, but don't worry, they don't hunt kids."

When I let go of Harry's jess, he took off like a rocket. In a split-second he was grasping the tube and banging it against a chair. But it was Rob's turn to look surprised, when he saw that I had no glove on my hand. He gave me a thumbs-up signal, and I knew right then that I could do this job. I felt triumphant.

I was aware of the hawk's talon strength, but it wasn't until later that I learned that they can exert 160 pounds of pressure. Somehow, that particular detail had not registered when I was preparing for my class. No wonder hawks have been used as hunters ever since humans figured out how to harness their abilities.

When I'd picked Harry up from his holding quarters that Monday before class, and stuck my ungloved hand into his cage, he'd alighted on my wrist gently and held on, tightening his talons but ever so gently, so I felt no pain, only little pin-pricks where the tip of each talon touched my skin. I exhaled and let go of the jess, but Harry just sat on my arm, stretching his reddish black wings as if he had nothing better to do.

CHAPTER 6

On the Way to Stardom

It was a brisk January day, the kind that felt bracing rather than freezing. In the zoo, the snow stayed white far longer than on the adjoining Bronx streets. I was blinded by it when I stepped out of my office. Although the day was sunny, I wore my favorite winter coat, an ankle-length sheepskin, the one I always thought had been at least partially responsible for getting me the job. The coat was honey-colored, with ornate, large gold buckles emerging from the creamy, curly trim that ran down the front. I felt like one of New York's glitterati wearing it, snuggled in its furry interior, and its warmth was a lifesaver over my low-cut mini dress that only reached to mid-thigh. Freedom of expression in fashion was the new catchphrase for women in the seventies, and mini dresses were all the rage.

I needed to look good that day because I was making my TV debut. If I didn't feel secure about my appearance, I'd have been a total wreck. Not only did I have to deliver wildlife information with flair and charm and no factual errors, I had to handle a live animal while looking perfectly at ease. Me—relaxed, holding a wild animal? That would surely sound like a joke to anyone who knew me, especially my neighbor Donna, who knew how scared I was of her Siamese cat. I had no idea when I took on the zoo job that it would occasionally require me to do television appearances. While such a possibility may have secretly thrilled me, I was rather shy and the very notion of speaking to untold numbers of viewers made me extremely nervous. Handling wild animals was daunting enough, but to have to do it with grace in front of cameras and lights made it downright terrifying.

Crunching through the snow, I made my way to our handleable animal holding facility, by now long closed for the season. Even when the Children's Zoo was open from spring through fall, this building was always closed to the public. I hadn't worked at the zoo long enough to have my own key, so I knocked. Kim opened the door and a familiar blast of warm air hit my face.

"Oh, it's so stuffy in here," I said, "The humidity will ruin my hair."

She rolled her eyes. "Don't sweat it," she said. "It's only the Captain Kangaroo show."

I was glad she had been informed by our PR office that I was to appear on the popular children's show, and hoped she'd have the animal ready and crated for me. I glanced at the wall clock and saw that I'd better hustle. It would be a disaster to show up late, and we still had a major hurdle ahead of us—getting me to the CBS Studios in Manhattan, with an animal.

In the seventies, the Bronx was well-known by taxi drivers as a danger zone. They avoided it like Thanksgiving with the in-laws, and their reluctance to service the area was not entirely unjustified. While there is no question that racial prejudice was a factor, at least three dozen drivers were killed in their cabs annually in the Bronx and other outer boroughs.

I asked Kim for the phone numbers of several taxi companies and started calling.

"Where did you say you need the cab?" the first dispatcher asked.

"The Bronx Zoo," I said. A brief moment of silence followed, then a burst of laughter. "No, seriously, I need a cab now," I said in my most assertive, professional manner. The guffaws continued.

I tried another taxi company. And another.

"Are you sure you want to go to the zoo on a cold day like today?" the fourth dispatcher asked. "I think they're closed anyway."

I started saying, "We never close… " but slammed the receiver down in frustration mid-sentence and glanced at the clock again. The fifth dispatcher sounded a tad more sympathetic.

"OK, lady, I'll be there in about twenty minutes."

"I'll have security open the back entrance," I said, an added bit of assurance that my call was neither a hoax nor a trap.

"Kim, is the ferret ready?" I asked.

"What ferret?" she said, looking mystified. "You're taking the boa."

"Who told you that?" I went weak in the knees and just stood there, biting my lip.

"The P.R. people. Bob Keeshan, the host, has built his entire program around a boa. You have to take Harriet," Kim said decisively.

I gulped. My heart was beating so fast it could have dribbled out of my chest, but I couldn't say anything. When I aced my job interview, it was assumed that I either knew how to handle animals or would be a quick study. Since it wasn't entirely clear what my duties would be, I hadn't even thought to inquire if animal handling was a part of the job. I wasn't about to blow my cover.

"OK," I said. "Let's put her in a case." Inside, my guts were twisting in primeval dread.

"What case?" Kim asked.

"You know, the carrying case," I said, trying to sound like an expert.

She looked at me. "Um, how long have you been working here? You should know that snakes go out in pillow cases."

At first I thought she was pulling my leg, but I saw her rifling through a pile of linens stacked in the corner of the stainless-steel counter.

"Shit," she said, "I don't have any of the big ones here. I just threw them into the washing machine." She pointed at the end of the building where the washer was spinning. I glanced at my watch and knew that if I didn't go out and wait for the cab at the gate, the driver would leave, thinking he had been duped.

"I've got to go," I said, panicked but trying to look calm. "I'll be late."

She opened the cage, reached in and took out Harriet, trying to balance her heft on both arms.

"Here, I have an idea," she said, and moved uncomfortably close. "Wrap her around your waist, like this." Before I could respond, she began draping the lethargic boa around my middle. "On a cold day like today she will hardly move." Kim looked like a fashion designer installing a new-fangled belt on a model. Then she said, "Perfect, your sheepskin coat will keep her cozy. It's better than a pillow case."

I was speechless.

"There, close those coat buckles and go." She moved on to another task.

I had no choice. Gingerly, I adjusted Harriet's smooth cool body and made sure her muscular bulk was evenly distributed around my waist. She felt nearly as heavy as my four-year-old son. For the moment, my nervousness about being late to the TV studio overshadowed my fear. I walked out toward the side entrance just as the security guard opened the metal gate and a yellow taxi skidded to a stop on the slippery entrance path.

The cabbie rolled down the window, looked me over from head to foot and whistled. "Let's go," he said, "Before the traffic gets any worse." I got into the back seat, inhaling an unidentifiable scent of air freshener fighting to overpower the tobacco stink. I hoped the odors wouldn't annoy Harriet, but she remained as inert as a thick brown belt. After the shock at my circumstance wore off a little, all I could think of was, if only Donna could see me here, sitting in a taxi with a huge serpent snuggled up to my belly, a regular Eve earning her daily bread.

Nah, she'd never believe it.

Unlike most New York City cabbies, this guy was not a talker. All he did was occasionally leer at me in the rear-view mirror. Our eyes met silently, and I knew better than to engage him in small talk. We drove past several of the Bronx streets that gave the otherwise lovely borough a bad name: boarded up windows, graffiti, overflowing garbage cans, seedy-looking men loitering in front of bodegas. When we got on the Sheridan Expressway, the Manhattan skyline rose before me like a mirage. Soon I'd be making my television debut. Anything was possible in this enchanted city.

I was so absorbed that I hadn't noticed how warm the cab had become. Little beads of perspiration began to form on my forehead. Harriet stirred, a little at first, then more. I felt her undulating movements along my waist like a strange massage. It was odd, but for a while my fear had mostly abated, but then I started wondering. When was she last fed a plump rat or freshly-killed chicken dinner? Could she be hungry? I visualized a boa skull with its needle-like rows of backward-pointed teeth that would not allow the prey to escape, its stretchy mouth ligaments that could take in an animal much larger than its head. She had me in the perfect position. Like any constrictor, all she had to do was tighten her grip until my lungs could no longer expand and take in air.

"It's very warm in here," I announced to the driver as we drove through midtown at last, getting close to my destination. "Any chance you can turn down the heat?" I asked urgently, because Harriet was now cruising around me and I worried she'd slither away. What would I do if she got stuck under the seat, or made her way into the trunk? Worse yet, she might slide up, reach my face and plunge her teeth into my cheek. The warmth had animated her; she must have thought she was in her tropical South American home again and my waist was a heck of a tree trunk. As soon as this ridiculous notion invaded my brain, I realized that I didn't really know if she had been collected in the wild or if she was captive bred. I knew that boas raised in captivity were more docile, but Harriet's provenance was a mystery. I began to sweat profusely and kept adjusting her around my middle. Then I noticed the driver glancing up at the rear-view mirror with a look of intense curiosity. Finally, he asked, "Hey, lady, whatcha got there?"

I didn't give it a moment's thought. I simply blurted out, "It's a boa constrictor."

In an instant the driver slammed on the brakes and shouted hysterically. "Get out, get out, right now!" Before I knew what had happened, he turned and reached for the handle on my door, opened it, screaming, "Now, now, now!"

I made a vain attempt to calm him and pay the fare, but he was so terrified, he looked as if he'd bust the blood vessel pulsating on his temple if I didn't make my exit. I clambered out onto the street and saw that he had come to a halt not on the roadway, but on the sidewalk. Oh my God, I thought. I could have gotten someone killed with my ill-timed confession.

Trying to regain composure, I gulped the cool air and looked around for the nearest street sign. I was lucky after all. My unceremonious ejection from the taxi took place only two blocks from the studio. Now somewhat calmed, I repositioned Harriet again and entered the lobby of the studio with five minutes to spare.

My heels made a tap-tapping sound on the polished marble floor, causing the guard at the reception desk to look up as I approached to sign in. I imagined his eyes resting on my middle. This time I'd know the answer. My ample coat to the rescue again. I'm pregnant, I'd say demurely.

Luckily, after this rocky preamble, the appearance on the show went off without a hitch, and Harriet made a big splash on the little screen.

◆◆◆

Not long after, Bob Keeshan, Captain Kangaroo himself, requested my appearance once again. Boy, I must be getting pretty good at this animal handling stuff, I thought. But I was forgetting how many of the critters I had yet to meet, up close and personal.

A call from Kim at the Children's Zoo holding facility confirmed the rumor I had heard the day before. "You're scheduled to be on set at eight-thirty tomorrow morning," she said, "Better get in real early to pick up your animals. You'll have to fight rush hour traffic." She hung up before I could ask which animals. As far as I knew, none of them were "mine."

Next morning I rose at the ungodly hour of five a.m. to make sure I got everything ready for the children before I dashed out to the zoo. I stopped in my office briefly so I could use our cramped ladies room to fix my hair, powder my nose, and apply lipstick. Looking at the mirror, I momentarily regretted my outfit choice, wondering if an animal would snag my black knit sweater with its claws, but that depended on which critters I would need to bring, something I still didn't know.

As I walked toward the Children's Zoo, one thought buzzed in my head. Alison, our P.R. manager, had remarked at lunch the day before that calls for television appearances were not very common, and it was a golden opportunity to highlight the zoo's collection and work on behalf of wildlife. "I hope they send a pro," she had said. "We can't afford to blow this. With spring around the corner, we can promote the reopening of the Children's Zoo."

How did I, still a novice in zoo biz, become the designated hitter? I had no idea. Luck?

The animal facility was buzzing with activity by the time I arrived, with instructors picking up critters to take to classes, keepers feeding the animals and cleaning holding cages, and the vet checking on some new arrivals. The first thing I heard upon entering was a keeper admonishing one of the instructors, "No, you can't take Dolly. She is going with Annette." Who's this Dolly? I thought. An animal I hadn't yet met? Or maybe a new instructor? I came around a bank of cages and saw Kim holding on her shoulder a narrow-bodied tan animal, about three feet long. Its two-foot tail was wrapped under Kim's arm and around her ribs.

"Who is this critter?" I asked, impressed by its extremely narrow head and wary little eyes.

"This is Dolly, the tamandua," Kim said. "Haven't you handled her yet?"

"No, I haven't," I said slowly, scanning my mental animal Rolodex. I had been up late the night before studying, reviewing, and preparing. I knew tamanduas were South American anteaters, but I hadn't realized they were this small. In my mind, they were closer to the size of their relatives, the giant anteater. Seeing a live animal is nothing like its picture. Weird in its thinness, Dolly's head scanned the area. She seemed very curious.

"Here, take her, she's a real sweetheart, just be careful of her claws." Kim began trying to disengage from Dolly. This was when I looked closer at Dolly's paw and noticed that one of her four digits was an enormous curved hook. My sweater will never survive this, I thought. Kim tried to hand Dolly over, but she clung to her with her powerful limbs. "Oh, she's feisty today," Kim remarked. "I hope she behaves for the cameras."

The transfer accomplished, Dolly was now on my shoulder, digging her claws into my sweater and my skin, too. Ugh, please God, careful of the sweater, Dolly girl, I thought. I judged her to be about six or seven pounds, but it wasn't her heft that worried me. It was those claws.

Kim brought out the holding cases and I struggled for a few moments, trying to get Dolly in without tearing my clothes to shreds. "Who else is going on the show today?" I asked.

"The Harris's hawk and the armadillo," she said.

"Good. I've handled those," I said. "But Dolly . . ." I hesitated.

"Don't worry. You'll do fine. Just play it by ear." Kim was being unusually outgoing. Maybe she was a morning person. But playing it by ear was never my *modus operandi*.

This time I wasn't taking a chance on using a taxi and having to explain the menagerie with me. Anyway, the cases were too large to fit into a trunk. Instead, Kim had arranged for the zoo van to drive me to the studios on Manhattan's west side. At seven-thirty in the morning, traffic was still bearable, but the driver must have seen me repeatedly glancing at my watch. "Don't worry, I'll get you there in plenty of time," he assured. Still, I fretted. I didn't want to embarrass the zoo by being late.

All through the drive I kept rehearsing my animal facts. Luckily, I knew that both armadillos and anteaters were members of the order *Edentata*, toothless New World insect eaters, so I could talk about their diets. I tried to visualize myself taking the creatures out of their cases smoothly, so as to give a professional impression. It occurred to me that all three of my stars had impressive claws, something else I could focus on. God help me if I let the hawk fly off my arm, or the three-banded armadillo scoot under some piece of furniture on its short legs. The little devil could be quick if he wanted to be. If he were frightened enough, he might roll up into a perfect armored cantaloupe and tumble to who knows where. And Dolly, well, she was my cross to bear for the day. I had no idea what pitfalls awaited me with her. I knew I'd manage, so long as they did not take place in front of the cameras.

Luckily, I had brought with me a "back up" star, a frisky ferret who could show off his ultra-bendable spine if I put him in the clear Plexiglas tube I carried with me. I knew that once I let him scamper inside it and closed off the far end, he would bend in half like a yogi and come back out the way he came in. Kids loved seeing that feat of flexibility in classes.

Upon arrival at the television studio building on 54th Street, I was met by three production assistants who helped bring the animals backstage. They bombarded me with questions as we rode up the service elevator. "Did you bring any predators?"

"Yes," I said nonchalantly.

"Anything that bites?" one of them asked, wide-eyed.

"Well, any animal can bite if provoked." I smiled at them, beginning to feel that, here, in a world of laypeople, I could be in command.

The production manager met me as soon as the animals had been placed backstage in their cases. "Did you bring the anteater?" he asked, before saying hello.

"Yes, I did," I replied.

"We want to be sure it shows its long tongue, so the kids can see it," he ordered.

I was mildly impressed that he knew about the storied foot-long anteater tongue, pink and skinny like cherry licorice.

"I can't guarantee that. Animals do what they want to do."

"This is show business. *We* know how to guarantee that," he said, smiling broadly, one upping me. "What does she eat?"

"If you mean Dolly, the anteater, she eats ants."

"This is Manhattan, honey," he said patronizingly, "We can get almost anything but ants."

Then he yelled to the assistants and instructed them to run downstairs. "Mike, Joe—fan out to the deli and grocery downstairs and bring up pickles, olives, mustard, and anything else spicy or strong-smelling for Dolly. We'll show her New York City hospitality."

I rolled my eyes. "Sounds delicious, but I am afraid she won't eat any of those delicacies," I said in my most polite voice.

"Dolly goes on in twenty-five. We shall see. Won't we?"

Here I'd been so concerned about the behavior of my animals, I hadn't considered the behavior of the studio executives. Silly me. Clearly, I needed more experience in this business, too.

Twenty long minutes later, Mike and Joe came huffing and puffing in with bags of groceries. They set out a dozen or more jars of assorted condiments, jams, and nibbles even I couldn't name. "Here boss, we got a bunch of choices for this finicky lady."

When the boss asked me to take Dolly out of her case, fortunately, she cooperated, though I sensed her nervousness as her claws became body-fat calipers, grasping chunks of skin on my back.

No sooner did I have her in my arms when the manager began shoving various jars under her long nose. "Here, here, you'll love this," he encouraged her, waving the jar of giant green olives under her tubular snout.

"You know, anteaters have no teeth, and if you noticed, her mouth is no wider than a pencil. She couldn't eat one of these even if she wanted to, and I assure you she doesn't."

He was not to be deterred. I doubted he heard anything I said. He continued to present Dolly with the other jars, some of which his assistants had trouble opening and I heard them cussing under their breath. Dolly was unmoved, but she began squirming in my arms and I worried what she'd do when I was called on stage with all those blaring lights. I knew that at any moment Dolly could activate the gland at the base of her tail and release a secretion whose stink is far worse than a skunk's—a revolting type of musk. I began to sweat in my black sweater, and the scratching of the ferret and armadillo in their cases made me even more uneasy.

Suddenly I heard the jaunty *Treasure House Keys* tune that announced the next show segment and heard the Captain himself announce, "Heeere comes our guest Dolly, and she is holding Annette. Let's give them both a round of applause." I walked onto the stage feeling a bit ridiculous to be called Dolly. After all, I looked nothing like Dolly Parton, who'd been a guest on the show, but the kiddies in the audience wouldn't know the difference.

Bob Keeshan—the Captain, with no ship to command— did have a huge and benign presence. In his red jacket with white piping around the collar and oversized kangaroo-style pockets, he was the very image of a kindly grandfather. The fringe of bangs framing his face softened his appearance with the signature walrus-like mustache. No wonder children responded to him. His gentle demeanor put me at ease as well. I was glad that the foods experiment hadn't worked out backstage, so I could show off Dolly's marvelous prehensile tail and her powerful arms capable of tearing up termite mounds. As for the foot-long sticky tongue she used to get at ants and termites, I could only describe it. She would not show it, although she behaved like a perfect lady.

The demonstrations of the Harris's hawk and the armadillo went as planned. There was no need to haul out my back-up ferret.

"Thank you Dolly, that was fascinating," Captain Kangaroo said as my segment ended. I smiled. There was no sense correcting him.

♦ ♦ ♦

I collected the animal cases and prepared to leave, feeling a mixture of relief, amusement, and irritation. On my way to the service elevator, the stage manager glared at me as if I were responsible for Dolly's shy tongue. "Next time," he said, "try to bring a more cooperative animal."

It was then I realized that the staff and the Captain were as clueless about human and animal creatures as I was about show business.

CHAPTER 7

Zoo Mom

My daughter Jessica wanted a pet. This was not a passing whim; she made it clear that she wanted one even more desperately than a vintage Barbie, a GI Joe, a Slinky, and a Lego set put together.

You would think that a mother who worked at the zoo would find this to be a natural and reasonable request. But when it came down to it, I was so overwhelmed by my demanding job and graduate studies that I could not bring myself to consider caring for another living thing. I'd recently started working on a master's degree in Educational Administration, because I needed to learn statistics so I could conduct program evaluations, a missing component of our programs. I didn't even want plants, which I had loved before throwing myself into the world of work. How much more trouble a pet would be than watering any number of ferns, African violets, or cacti! It was all I could do to get out of the house at 8 a.m.

after hastily preparing lunches, throwing in a load of laundry, and hugging my children goodbye.

I knew that a pet would entail even more work, and that I could not in good conscience rely on a seven-year-old and her five-year-old brother to do it all. So, despite frequent protests of, "Yes, Mommy, I *would* feed it and change its water," I resisted.

There were days when I was seized with doubt and guilt. Every working parent, moms especially, wants to compensate for being away from home by allowing little luxuries and treats for their children, if we can afford them. And while I worked at a zoo and had plenty of animals to enjoy day in and day out, my daughter did not, and what was worse, many of her friends had pets ranging from adorable puppies and kitties to more exotic iguanas and turtles. Each time she would tell me of a visit to a friend's home and an encounter with a pet, my heart sank, but I held fast to my "no pets" edict.

As someone whose job was to educate the public about the responsible care of the world's fauna and endangered species, I wanted to honor my professional obligations. I knew that the day a new pet is brought home is a day for jubilation and excitement, but that all too soon that turns into indifference or worse. Once the pet is no longer a novelty, and cleaning its cage becomes an annoying intrusion on more fun activities, it is often neglected.

Some parents then resort to calling the zoo. "My Johnny can no longer care for his wonderful turtle, so we'd like to donate it to the zoo," they say, hoping for an enthusiastic response.

"Sorry, we don't accept animal donations. It is our policy."

"But why? It is a wonderful animal," they say, appalled.

Then we need to explain the zoo's concerns about disease transmission, space and funding limitations, and the importance of priority species. The calls become more urgent and numerous after Christmas and Easter, when children have grown tired of their puppies, chicks, and bunnies. I certainly would never be among such callers. We would avoid getting a pet in the first place. But our daughter had other ideas.

◆◆◆

By the spring just before her eighth birthday, the pet idea had gained gale-force strength. She came home one day bubbling with excitement. "Mom, our class is having a pet show," she said, eyes shining and her cheeks flushed pink.

"A pet show? What do you mean?" I asked.

"Mrs. Jaffee said that every kid should bring in their pet and have a speech prepared about its habits. It has to be really good, you know, because we will present it to the whole school! And parents will come too, and grandparents, and anyone we want to invite." Her torrent of words washed over me.

That teacher sure has nerve, I thought. "What about the children who have no pets?" I asked, chopping the onions for dinner.

"Well…" my daughter hesitated. "They can borrow a pet from a neighbor or a relative, I guess, I'm not real sure."

"How about doing library research and then presenting that?" I asked, searching my mind for a way around this annoying assignment.

"But Mom . . ."

"What?" I said, hoping that the tears that were welling in her blue eyes were from the onions.

"You are a *zoo mom*. Everyone in my class knows that. I'll be so embarrassed if I'm the only one without a pet!"

With that she ran into her room. Her dramatic sobs began to erode my resolve, and I knocked on her door. No answer. "I'll think about this, OK?" I said, loud enough for her to hear.

That night as I went to bed I thought about my daughter's predicament. I imagined the snickers of the boys in her class, the titters of the girls. I couldn't let that happen. What pet could we get that would not add to the animal tragedies I knew from my work? Endangered or threatened species of any sort were clearly out of the question, so what else? She loved kittens, but no, her dad was allergic and cats allowed to roam outdoors were responsible for the demise of thousands of wild birds. Fish? Too cold and impersonal, and too much hassle to constantly empty and clean the aquarium and get the water temperature just right.

Then my mind spun back to birds. I remembered how fascinated my daughter was with the blue jays in our yard, and how she loved my explanation that their feather color was just an optical illusion, not a pigment. "If you hold up a blue jay feather to light and look through it, it'll be just grey," I had said, and she had stood there, agape. Yes, I wanted her new pet to provide such teachable moments.

My husband was already asleep when I turned out the light. His rhythmic breathing made me calmer. I knew he'd support any decision I made on the pet question—after all, animals were my territory— but his long hours would not allow him to care for it. He rolled over in his sleep and touched my arm and suddenly I had my answer: budgies! They are monogamous and the males feed the female while she incubates her eggs. Their behavior reflected David's nurturing side. And the more I thought about these colorful Australian birds, the fonder I grew of the idea. They are talkative—just like Jessica—and they can be finger-tamed when they are young. The bird could keep her company after school, and we'd have a way to recycle all those weekend editions of *The New York Times* on the bottom of the cage. Before long, I'd convinced myself it was totally reasonable, maybe even a good idea.

When I told her at breakfast the next day, she was triumphant. "Oh, Mommy, I will prepare the best presentation for the show. You won't be disappointed," she grinned from ear to ear, and I instantly felt like Mother of the Year.

That weekend, we set out for the pet shop. One of the birds seemed very curious when he saw her. She watched with fascination as he hopped over to investigate her and cocked his little head in a way I knew would make him the winner over his cage mates.

After we brought him home, there was a lot of excitement setting up the cage with perches and seed dishes, along with a few heated arguments over what to name the bird. "He's green like a lime," Jessica, the main owner, pronounced. "I will call him Lime."

"No," her brother claimed part ownership. "Don't you see the yellow parts, his head and the spot on his chest? I want to call him Lemon."

"OK, Lemon-Lime it is," I said.

They both smiled—that settled that.

◆ ◆ ◆

Two weeks before the pet show, a parent-teacher conference was scheduled. I was glad the school, P.S. 95, was close to our home. I had so much work that I had brought some home—strategic plans and next year's budget—that I needed to finish that night. It was a chilly four-block walk. I stepped into the school building that smelled of chalk and tuna fish sandwiches, and was glad to be indoors. I walked down the long corridor to Room 217, where about a dozen parents had already gathered. Mrs. Jaffee sat at her desk, organizing a stack of papers, but as soon as I walked in she looked up and greeted me.

"Before we get started, I must say something to you, Mrs. B, and the others may as well listen," she said.

"What is it?" I asked, feeling uncomfortable.

She smiled a wide smile showing her very white teeth. "It's about your daughter."

I said, "Oh?" and searched my memory of what it could possibly be—her lost tooth, her uneaten lunch?—and wondered why the other parents need to be involved.

"Your daughter is unbelievably creative," Mrs. Jaffee said.

"Is it her drawings?" I asked, thinking of an art project the class did—it was nice enough, though hardly exceptional.

"No, it was for science class," she said.

I knitted my brows, "I know she's a terrific reader, but science...?"

"It's that inspired idea she came up with for a pet show," the teacher said. "I encouraged the children to come up with suggestions for an end-of-semester project."

I looked at Mrs. Jaffee's animated face and nodded, trying to absorb this revelation. "The class loved her idea best. I've never seen so much excitement," she continued.

Just then an image of my daughter flashed before me. It was the day she came home from kindergarten, excited when she first learned the Pledge of Allegiance. "But, Mommy, I didn't say 'under God,' I said 'under Mother Nature,'" she told me. I smiled inside, admiring her ingenuity.

"Oh, the pet show," is all I could say. I may have been had, but I was still proud. "Thank you for the compliment, Mrs. Jaffee. She *is* a rare bird."

◆ ◆ ◆

Now that Jessica had her bird, her younger brother, tired of being just a part-owner, wanted a pet of his own. Their sibling rivalry reminded me of the spirited chases and fights among primate offspring.

And again, that working-mom guilt rose up in me. One of the reasons I think my kids didn't seem to mind my going to work when they were still quite young was that they imagined my job was like play. "You get to go to the zoo every day. *You are so lucky*," they'd say. And it was true—I did feel fortunate to go each day to a place that was bursting with life, where I could see and sometimes hold adorable animals, from baby monkeys to newborn cheetah cubs. It was thrilling that each day brought new knowledge, new experiences, and a growing sense that I was doing something to leave a better world for my children. None of this heady feeling, however, meant the job was easy. I worked long hours. Sometimes my friends would be incredulous that I couldn't get home in time to feed my children dinner, a task that often fell to my husband. "You aren't a doctor, after all… " they'd say. But we were doing something important: we were saving the world, the animal world at least, I wanted to tell them in moments of weary, overworked, adrenaline-fueled grandeur. We were a team, Team Wildlife: me and my group of talented colleagues. We struggled to meet publishing deadlines, putting all our energies and ingenuity into designing programs to inspire a love of nature. When we were finishing a book or a teachers' manual that had to go to press, we'd leave the office at eight, nine, ten o'clock—after many calls from my children asking if I was on my way. So it wasn't quite the kind of play my kids had in mind.

Like many working mothers, I felt guilty at times about not being there when they came home from school to find a babysitter instead of a mom who had baked chocolate chip cookies. But I did my best to make it up to them, with trips to the zoo with behind-the-scenes access, museum outings, play dates, big birthday parties, Disney vacations, and summer camps. But by the time my son reached the ripe old age of seven, it was clear that my efforts to provide fun and amusement did not quite measure up. "Mommy, all I want is a pet," he pleaded.

He spoke wistfully about his friends' pets, and when he did, his blue eyes shone with excitement, so after a while he wore me down. Now the only issue was to select an easy-to-care-for animal, one that would provide those teachable moments. It was my son's luck to be stuck with a teacher mom, but as least I wasn't planning any tests! We went to the library and scoured the animal books. He looked at pictures of the old standbys—dogs, cats, gerbils—but with each one I found a reason why it may not be the ideal companion. Eventually I said, "Let's find you something different, a pet that will stand out from those of your friends."

He looked at me questioningly. "Like what, mom? A dinosaur?"

Huh. Now that was an idea.

I jumped off my chair and pulled him toward the arthropod shelf in the library. "I have an idea that'll blow your socks off," I said enthusiastically, as if I were trying to sell him a used car.

"I'm not even wearing any socks," he said, but I could tell that he was intrigued. I shuffled through the books because an idea of the ideal pet had finally dawned on me. But my son was beginning to get restless. "What kind of an animal is it, Mom?" he asked.

"OK, I'll give you a clue and see if you can figure it out."

He seemed only moderately interested, but willing. "So, what's the clue?"

"Well, its skeleton is not like ours, on the inside."

"Where is it?" I could see a little twinkle in his eyes.

"It's on the outside of its body."

"Mom, that's not enough. I need another clue." He scrunched his face with effort.

"It breathes through gills, but it's not a fish." He looked very confused, so I decided to stop the charade. "OK, it's a hermit crab."

"A what?"

"You heard me. It's a crab, a very cool animal that lives in a shell, with an enormous claw and eyes that rotate on stalks." Now he looked very interested, so I persisted. "It's a cousin to a scorpion."

"Wow, Mom, can I have it? Can I?"

"Sold," I said, "if you promise to take good care of it. We'll get a couple of them because they are very sociable." Now a huge smile bloomed on his face.

True to my promise, the following week we purchased two small hermit crabs and outfitted their terrarium with sand, shells of various sizes, and some plastic climbing toys. I told Jeremy that as they grew the crabs would move into ever-larger discarded snail shells to protect their delicate bellies. He named the larger of the two critters Hermie and the smaller Crabby. Hermie quickly became his favorite. He watched the hermit crabs with the patience of a scientist and couldn't wait to present his pets as part of his science show-and-tell. He became the envy of his friends, whose pets did not have scary-looking claws that could crush a coconut, or compound eyes with many lenses. Hermie's anatomy seemed closer to a space alien than an ordinary dog or kitten, and that was worth everything.

I figured that once he lost interest in these crustaceans, my contribution to their care would be nominal. I had a warm feeling of satisfaction that I had managed to respond to my son's request with such a relatively simple solution.

Weeks and months passed, but Jeremy did not lose interest in the hermit crabs. He was diligent about putting fresh water in their dish and feeding them pieces of fruit, bits of lettuce, and cracker crumbs. He loved to watch them eat and often called to us, "Come here, you have to see something." He could sit for hours observing the two crabs crawling around on the floor. Sometimes he staged crab races, but since Hermie was bigger he always won. After a while the game became pointless.

Eventually both hermit crabs grew, molted, and moved into larger shells, but Crabby's growth overtook Hermie's. When Crabby outgrew the largest shell we had, we placed a small metal can in the terrarium for him to move into, but our son felt it wasn't quite right. "Mom, we've got to find a bigger shell," he pleaded.

"I have already tried the largest ones I could find, but he didn't like them."

"Why is he so choosy?"

"Animals have preferences too. You might not like to live in any old house," I said.

Eventually, I took Crabby to the zoo to be adopted by someone with more expertise in his care. Now Hermie was a lone crab, and our son's love affair with him continued, although he worried about what would happen if we could no longer provide a larger shell.

From the babysitter's reports, I knew that my son headed straight for Hermie's terrarium every day after school, before getting his own snack, to feed and visit with his pet.

◆ ◆ ◆

I was at work in an important meeting one day when my secretary burst into my office and said, "Your son is on the phone."

"Well, didn't you tell him I was busy? I'll call him when the meeting is over, Mary."

"You need to speak with him now," she said solemnly.

"Why? What happened?"

"He's crying. He's hysterical."

"Oh, my God, put him right through," I said, guilt and concern heating my face. She did as I asked, but all I could hear at first was his blubbering. I couldn't make out what he was saying. "Now, take a deep breath, blow your nose, and tell me what happened." The crying subsided enough so that I could make out some words in between his sharp gulps of air.

"He, he... he... he's dead."

"Slow down. Who is dead?" A knot formed in the pit of my stomach as I imagined the possibilities. There was a momentary silence, followed by another burst of sobbing.

"Please, honey, try to calm down and tell me again," I pleaded now.

"It... it... it's Her... Her... Hermie," he finally choked out, to my great relief. I felt a sudden urge to chuckle at his deep attachment to a creature so cold-blooded and ungainly, but remembered that his Hermie was not so different from my old pal, Bully. One of the reasons why I had agreed to a pet in the first place was to help him learn about life's lessons, and how could I forget that the death of a loved one is one of them?

I needed to come up with something smart and soothing. Frantically, I searched for the right words, but I felt too much pressure with my colleagues staring at me. I blurted out, "But it was just a crab. Hermie really didn't know you." Instantly, I wanted to choke back the words. I couldn't have come up with a stupider attempt at consolation. For a moment, I must've forgotten he was only seven.

A moment of silence hung suspended in the air. Then, the sound of his heavy breathing alternating with noisy sniffles broke my heart. He was probably sitting in front of the terrarium, his wet nose pressed against the glass, staring at his inert after-school buddy. I imagined his little scrunched face with snot bubbles running down, mixing with tears. While I sat there beating myself up over my insensitive remark, he composed himself a little and managed to say, "But, Mommy, I... I... loved him like, like my own... son."

Of course, I knew what he meant. This was his first encounter with death, so I had to work hard to keep from showing my amusement at the way he put it. It was both heart-wrenching and oddly reassuring to see a child develop so much affinity for the most uncuddly of pets.

"You calm down, OK? I'm on my way home," I said. "I'm bringing you a hug and some Ring Dings." That seemed to do the trick.

"Can we bury Hermie in the backyard?" he asked, now calmer.

"OK. When dad gets home."

I apologized to my colleagues, who had witnessed the entire episode, and ran to the parking lot to get home as quickly as possible.

As I drove home I went over and over all the possible causes of Hermie's demise. Was the humidity in our house too low? Did our water have traces of chlorine in it? Had we missed a vital component of his diet? Or maybe, as a social animal, he had died of a broken heart once his terrarium mate was gone. The questions spun around in my head. I tried to determine if I had failed to provide my son with a piece of vital information on hermit crab care. As I approached my exit, I decided to stop obsessing.

After all, I had a funeral to attend.

CHAPTER 8

Briggs and Zishe: Males of Steel

I never met Briggs in person, and there aren't too many people alive today who actually knew him. Sometimes memories become distorted by time, but luckily in this case, I located the man who remembers the incident best—James Doherty, the Bronx Zoo's General Curator at the time. You'll have to take his word for it, as unbelievable as this story will sound. Actually, the story of the other protagonist of this chapter, Zishe, is equally unbelievable.

Bodybuilding is big business today: six-pack abs sell everything from beer to deodorant, and the sale of exercise equipment generates billions. But it wasn't always this way, especially in pre-WWII Europe, when the great majority of people were more preoccupied with just surviving. When I was a young girl growing up in Poland, my father fascinated me with stories of a mythical strongman named Zishe. The tales were so fantastic, so unreal, that I thought of them as fairytales, and he recounted them as if they were. "*Ania, aza min oysergeveyndlikhe mensch, dos iz nisht tsu farshteyen*," he'd say to me in Yiddish. "Such an exceptional man, it is not something that can be understood." He told me how Zishe could drive a spike into a five-inch oak slab with a single smack of his palm; bend thick iron bars into flowers; tear apart metal chains with his teeth as if they were made of spider web silk; take on six burly men, each twice his weight, and knock them out in minutes, and even pull a wagon filled with several full grown men with his jaw. To my father and me, Zishe was the very definition of strength.

I never tired of those stories. No wonder he was hailed as the Strongest Man in the World, no small feat for a Jew, since Eastern European Jews of that era were thought to be small, weak, and more interested in books than physical feats.

How did my father know about Zishe? He'd tell me that when he was a young boy, a *klein yingl*, a legendary man named Zishe would walk through the courtyards of impoverished Lodz tenements and demonstrate his amazing power. "Did you actually see him in person?" I'd ask.

"When I was a very small," he'd say, with a faraway look in his eyes. "Mostly, I heard about his feats of strength from people in the neighborhood and those who traveled to the *shtetls* where he performed."

◆◆◆

As an adult, I had all but forgotten about Zishe until I began working at the zoo and observed the orangutans. Those magnificent red-haired primates, who share 97% of their genetic heritage with us, captivated me. It's no surprise that Indonesians named them the way they did: *orang-hutan* means "forest person" in the Malay language. Orangutans' intelligence and ability to use tools is bolstered by their grasping toes as well as their hands. While we pride ourselves, evolutionarily speaking, on our opposable thumbs that enable exquisite dexterity, orangs have opposable big toes as well as opposable thumbs! Researchers have observed them using as many as fifty-four different tools to extract insects for meals, and twenty more for consuming fruit. They are known to use leafy branches as umbrellas and large folded leaves as cups. Orang mothers keep their young with them until they are about seven or eight years old and teach them survival skills.

Today the biggest threat to orangs, who have few predators other than humans, are poachers who, despite strict laws, kill the mothers and steal the youngsters to sell to people who want them as pets. Gone are the days at the beginning of the twentieth century when orangs at zoos were dressed in little outfits to sit and have lunch with the children of the privileged. Today's Wildlife Conservation Society has a Wildlife Crimes Unit which, in collaboration with Indonesian authorities, has confiscated and reintroduced to the wild over 150 orangs that were held as pets under inhumane conditions. Poaching is a problem, but indiscriminate cutting of their forest home is just as serious a threat. Large tracts of rainforest are cut to grow palm oil trees, contributing to the orangutans' critical status.

But despite their endangered status, what stands out to me the most is the legendary strength of these gentle creatures. Some scientists have estimated an adult male orang's strength to be seven times that of a human male of comparable weight, a trait that helps them navigate by swinging and leaping through the branches of rainforests in Sumatra and Borneo. Sometimes, when observing the zoo orangs, I've wondered how they'd do in a competition with Zishe. Both relied on natural physical prowess and not on fancy conditioning regimens, machines, or steroids. Yet in my mind, Zishe was always a figment of my father's imagination, while Briggs the zoo orang, with his intense eyes and ruddy hair, was unmistakably real.

One day, while browsing through a second-hand bookshop, I came across a book about Zishe. To my amazement, he was a flesh-and-blood man. He actually existed! He was a sensation in Europe in the early twenties, and not just that— he arrived in America in 1923 and performed his feats before an audience of thousands. It became clear to me that when my father recounted the strongman stories it had been nearly forty years since he had seen or heard aboutZishe's performances as a very young boy, so they acquired a dream-like quality. I even found a children's book about Zishe. He was as real and probably just as strong as Briggs, the Bronx zoo orang, or at least that is how I envisioned them both: a Superman of the city and one of the forest.

Though I did not witness the amazing strength of either, I did hear a keeper, an old-timer, say that one day Briggs got tired of sitting in his cage, which back then was just that, not a habitat environment like we have today. James Doherty, the General Curator at the time, told me about this one-of-a-kind incident that showed how Briggs was not only extraordinarily strong, he was equally smart.

While the Ape House was being remodeled, shifting animals for cleaning and feeding was a challenge. One day, a keeper was feeding Briggs through a partially-open cage door. Suddenly, Briggs slapped the door open all the way and ran out. The keeper jumped up and closed the security door to keep Briggs in the keeper alley. Briggs proceeded to tip over the refrigerator; drink about a case of canned milk by biting through the cans; eat whatever he could find of his favorite treats: apples, bananas, eggs, and biscuits; and break a bunch of light bulbs before being tranquilized. After the remodeling, Briggs took apart the light fixtures in the ceiling and their wiring, although they were the kind used in prisons, designed to resist tampering. And if he really wanted to, he could take apart his cage using only his fingernails.

I can imagine him simply picking up the entire refrigerator and walking out, hugging it to his chest! If the keepers hadn't spotted him, he would have been the first orang to ever hawk appliances on the corner of Fordham Road and Southern Boulevard.

CHAPTER 9

Cattitude

When I was five years old, my family spent the summer in a country village in Poland. One morning I awoke to cries and laments coming from the tiny, thatched-roof cottage across the way. I ran out barefoot in my nightie to find old women in babushkas standing around crying and bemoaning the loss of their friend, an old woman who had died during the night.

"Would you believe it?" one asked. "Her cat was sitting on her chest when she was found."

"It's just like a cat," another responded, "Cats steal your breath. They kill silently."

I was overwhelmed. The orange kitty with dark stripes I had seen around the dead woman's house was a killer! I ran back home and cried for hours, refusing to tell anyone why. Would I die if the cat came near me? For several days, the orange tabby came to me in nightmares, leaving me terrorized and drenched in sweat.

What a long-lasting, unhealthy impact that experience had on me. I had carried this Old-World superstition around with me for so long, I hardly thought about it. My fearful response to domestic cats became instinctive.

It was my friendship with my wonderful neighbor Donna and her household coterie of guests, human and animal, that eventually rehabilitated me. Donna had a Seal Point Siamese named Percival, affectionately known as Percy. With his regal posture, caramel coat, and watchful blue eyes, he exemplified the best in domestic cat-dom, except that his manners were still decidedly wild. Every time I crossed Donna's threshold, before she learned to banish him to the bedroom during my visits, he stalked me, his taut haunches looking as if he were about to pounce. I was sure his hissing augured an imminent attack.

Percy's behavior was a legacy of Donna's frontier life on the wild western side of Vancouver Island in British Columbia, where he spent most of his time outdoors, fending for himself. Donna told me how he would triumphantly bring her birds, squirrels, and baby rabbits. Each time she bragged about Percival's hunting skills, I'd think of the Heads and Horns collection of trophies—white rhino, Marco Polo sheep, musk ox— contributed by record-holders and once hidden in my Education Building. Ironically, some of the Great White Hunters, such as Teddy Roosevelt and Ernest Hemingway, were guided on their hunts in Kenya by a skilled guide named Philip Hope Percival. Donna's Percy's history as a hunter was memorialized in his sleek body, its finely-carved muscles and old battle scars. But all he could do now was sit by the windows in his Bronx home and watch birds on the fire escape while he licked his chops.

Despite, or perhaps because of his fine feline features, Percy terrified me. Before I'd walk into her apartment to visit and share endless cups of black coffee, Donna would lock him up in the bedroom. "Annette, you'd get used to Percy if you let me keep him in the living room even for a little while," she would suggest.

"Maybe next time," was all I could manage each time.

Soon enough, I had two reasons to feel uncomfortable in Donna's apartment: Percy, the cat and Frenchie, her ex-con houseguest. Frenchie had been incarcerated in the notorious Attica prison. It was the 1970s, and Donna was a crusader for a number of liberal causes. She was at the forefront of a movement to rehabilitate African American ex-cons who had not been given access to qualified legal defense and who claimed innocence. Due to Donna's tireless efforts, Frenchie had gone to art school and was now a budding artist employed in a lithography studio. He was a small, wiry man with glistening biceps in his taut arms. One could easily imagine he had had no trouble defending himself from assaults by other inmates. The only thing that softened his hard appearance was a black wool beret cocked on his abundant afro. Even though I admired Donna for giving Frenchie temporary shelter, I couldn't help feeling a bit guarded and wary of his criminal past. I wondered what his alleged crime had been, but wasn't sure I wanted to know the answer.

Donna's apartment was across the hall from ours, and in those days we kept our doors unlocked and frequently borrowed cooking supplies from one another. Because of our open-door policy, she let me know as she was stepping out one day that Frenchie would still be there. She had found him a place to live, she said, but he wouldn't be leaving until the next day.

Later that day, I realized I had left my glasses at Donna's after our morning coffee. I didn't want to disturb Frenchie, but I needed them to read a recipe. I crossed the small landing and knocked softly on the door. No use surprising Frenchie, I thought. No answer. I knocked harder. Still no answer. I opened the door cautiously and scanned the room for Percy. He was nowhere in sight.

"Anyone here?" I called out.

A barely audible voice came from behind a closed bedroom door. This was the bedroom of Donna's seven-year-old twins, who were at school. I approached the bedroom door, put my ear against it and listened. Silence. I knocked again. "I'm here," a man's faint voice reached my ears. I opened the door cautiously.

To my total shock, Frenchie was cowering on the topmost bunk bed, covered by a child's patchwork quilt with frolicking bears on it. All I could see were his wary eyes beneath his beret, which was askew.

"Is he here?" Frenchie whispered, and moved further into the corner, squashing a large pink rabbit.

"Who?" I asked, mystified.

"Percy!"

"The cat?"

"Yeah, that devil creature with evil eyes."

I looked around nervously and didn't see Percy. "No, I don't see him."

"Well, I ain't gettin' down until Donna's home and gets him away from me."

I couldn't believe my ears. This tough guy was as frightened of Percy as I was, maybe more. I wanted to burst out laughing, but thought better of it.

"OK, have it your way," I said. "I'm just here to get my glasses."

With that Frenchie dove under the quilt, where he'd remain for the next few hours. "Close the bedroom door tight when you leave," he muttered as I made my exit.

◆ ◆ ◆

That evening I couldn't shake the image of Frenchie trembling, huddled under the blanket in mortal panic over a cat. I wondered how he had acquired his fear. Had a voodoo cat taunted his childhood? I knew where my fear had originated. If Frenchie looked so ridiculous frightened by a ball of fur, I must appear exactly that way. The thought embarrassed me. I wondered if I could ever stop sprinting across the street when I saw a cat sauntering up the block.

It was late. I rubbed my eyes and went to bed promising myself to try to relax around those creatures most people thought of as mere pussy cats. Was there a reform school for lost cases like Frenchie and me? Maybe I could start by not insisting that Donna lock Percy up every time I entered her apartment, so he wouldn't be mewling pitifully the whole time.

But change can be slow. Gradually, I allowed Percy to remain in his living room, but I still was frozen in fear when he slinked past me and swiped his sinuous tail against my leg.

◆◆◆

By the time my department acquired Carlos, a puma (also known as a mountain lion, panther or cougar), my fear of domestic cats had been somewhat tempered with reason, although they could still send shivers down my spine. To be perfectly honest, I still try to avoid domestic cats.

But Carlos elicited an entirely different response. Noble in his bearing, Carlos was a stunningly beautiful animal with alluring green, almond-shaped eyes, rippling muscles, and soft, tawny fur. In many ways, Percy was a miniature of the puma, but Carlos was wild. Maybe it was his wildness and the possibility of danger, the romance of getting so close to a powerful predator or his penetrating gaze, but I fell head over heels in love with him. Like any love, there was no rationale and no explanation for it. My fear seemed to evaporate after I learned to handle him properly. The process was gradual, but still faster than befriending Percy.

The first time the mammal keeper brought him to our office, I backed away, nearly arching my back like a frightened cat. Carlos yawned and showed me his impressive canines. "Ooh, not a cavity in sight, you'd make my dentist happy,"

I said to myself. "This office must bore you, with no trees to climb. Are you in need of lunch, big kitty?" I wanted to ask him, but his eyes were hypnotic. "He is young still and trainable," the keeper said. "If you have patience he'll be your big kitty in no time." My big kitty? I'd never yearned for one, but the challenge in his comment made me brave. "Show me how to handle him," I said, as if that was all I needed.

Carlos was the quintessential American cat. Scientists have recorded the presence of his species from southern Canada all the way to the tip of South America. The keeper told me that animal authorities had confiscated Carlos from an unscrupulous "pet" owner who purchased him illegally. The young cat arrived at the Bronx Zoo tame, but in poor health and in need of nurturing by veterinary staff. After attending to his medical needs and feeding him a healthy carnivore diet, the vets turned him over to the Education Department to use in classes.

In the wild, his strong and muscular hind legs and large paws would have allowed him to climb with great agility over rocks, where he'd be hunting rabbits, raccoons, even sheep, goats, and pigs. At the zoo, he had to be satisfied with a commercial carnivore mix and the occasional beef shank bone. But it was those incredible hind legs that made Carlos a star in our classes.

No matter how rowdy a group I may have been teaching, the moment I announced that a mountain lion was about to make an appearance, the immediate murmur of anticipation would be followed by an awed hush. Unencumbered by a leash or any restraint, Carlos would saunter in silently and scan the room's mesmerized faces with the hyper vigilance of a top predator. Even though I had promised not to bring out any animal that would harm them, the students sat breathless and a bit frightened. They treated Carlos with more respect than they accorded many of their teachers. With his acute hearing, Carlos reacted to even the smallest shuffle: a child moving his legs or shifting in a chair. He was a cooperative teaching assistant and made it easy to illustrate all the points I wanted to make about the exquisite adaptations he had for a predatory life style.

After the students relaxed a bit and were reassured that they would not become Carlos's lunch, they began to timidly raise their hands. I was delighted to answer their questions and delve deeper into the life history of this magnificent cat. Most of all, I wanted to convince them that killing mountain lions was wrong, that these wonderful creatures were doing a necessary job in their ecosystem of keeping their prey populations—like deer, rabbits and coyotes— in check. It was easy to see the glint of comprehension in the children's eyes, and as a teacher, I knew that it might not have been possible without Carlos right there before them.

I wanted the children to know how habitat destruction and hunting have reduced the number of wild cats worldwide, so most are severely endangered. Years later, I'd come across this statistic: from 1996 to 2006, 30,000 pumas were shot in the United States. With shrinking wilderness, there are the inevitable intrusions by pumas into populated areas, that's why educating the public about them is so important. And there was no better way to make an impression than a live appearance.

I'd say, "Can you all promise not to move, yell, or jump? If you can, I will show you one more of his amazing features."

"Yes, yes," they'd respond in unison.

"Do you remember what I said about his strong back legs?"

"Yes," they nodded knowingly.

"OK, then, sit still."

At that point I would let Carlos go and he would make a nearly thirty-foot leap from the front of the auditorium to the back, where another instructor had held up a treat. The children would be awed, their mouths hanging open in disbelief of what they had just witnessed. They'd sit still, momentarily absorbing the animal's athletic feat.

"They can jump up as high as fifteen feet and leap forward as far as forty feet,"

I'd say, ending the class with Carlos still licking his chops in the back.

◆◆◆

When Carlos belonged to our collection of "education animals" he was still a youngster and weighed less than fifty pounds, but as he grew larger we could no longer handle him safely. The entire staff of my department was saddened the day Carlos was moved to the cat house with his feline brethren. He had graduated from Education and now played his part as a Lion House exhibit specimen, where he attracted a great deal of attention from the public.

When it was built in 1903, The Lion House, a majestic 20,000 square-foot Beaux Arts building, was a state-of-the-art exhibit with skylights and a sophisticated underground mechanism for shifting animals from one cage to another. But by the early eighties it was sorely out-of-date, not fit to illustrate anything of interest about Carlos's wild habitat. Carlos spent his days pacing the small outdoor cage. When I saw him napping on the cement floor, twitching his whiskers, I wondered if he was dreaming of his days as teacher's assistant and the freedom to leap for a treat. Now a mature male, he must have weighed at least 130 pounds. Despite the bare cage, visitors enjoyed watching Carlos, but he did not seem to be enjoying them and often turned around abruptly, waving his impressive, three-foot tail as if to say, "I've had enough of your ogling."

For the most part, animal exhibits attract people who love wild creatures and nature, but there are the occasional misfits who pose as visitors. One day an unusually mean teenager taunted Carlos with a towel. Why anyone would bring a towel to the zoo is a mystery. Perhaps he had used it in a nearby pool. People who witnessed the scene reported that he waved the towel across the cage's bars, back and forth, in a vain attempt to instigate a response from Carlos. The cat looked up lethargically and ignored the teenager. Enraged that Carlos had disregarded his taunts, the teen swatted the towel forcefully at the cage. The limp cloth slipped between the bars and landed on the enclosure's cement floor with a thud. Disgusted, the surly young man skulked away.

For a while after this incident, no one knew why Carlos refused to eat. He appeared sicker each day, laying pathetically still, not bothering to even swat at flies with his luxurious tail. After a few days, the keepers transferred him to the animal hospital. There, the vet found out what had happened: Carlos had swallowed the towel and suffered a serious obstruction of his intestines. He died shortly after, despite the vet's heroic efforts to save him. No one in my division was more heartbroken than I was. Intellectually, I know that the loss of a single animal in the face of huge wildlife losses is insignificant; yet, to me, Carlos will always be the only kitty who had me at hello. Many years have passed and I still miss that proud cat.

Remembering Carlos always makes me think of another puma at the Bronx Zoo. The zoo's first director, William T. Hornaday, had kept a pet puma that was a gift from a Mexican zoo. One day in the summer of 1902, the puma escaped from the well-fortified box in which he was kept. The cat ran through the zoo's grounds with abandon, frightening groups of picnickers and devouring their sandwiches. All efforts to recapture the puma failed and eventually it took a leap into a chestnut tree, from which it later jumped into the Bronx River and swam to freedom. After an exhaustive search yielded no results, Mr. Hornaday assured the press the cat would not harm anyone. To the best of anyone's knowledge, the cat was never found and most likely disappeared into the forested areas of New York state.

Knowing Carlos as I did, I couldn't help but think he'd have made a similar dash if given half a chance.

CHAPTER 10

A Very Big Worm

My boss Tom lived at the zoo. It took me a long time to get used to the idea of working at the zoo, so having a boss who lived there seemed like a joke at first. When I'd tell my friends that he lived at the zoo they'd invariably come back with, "In a cage?" Then I'd explain that no, it wasn't a cage at all and that in a modern zoo we didn't call them cages anyway—they were exhibits, or enclosures. "Okay, whatever," they'd say. "Which enclosure does he live in?"

The zoo and my very job there also inspired countless quips that people thought were clever. My first job as a zoo instructor elicited an almost ubiquitous giggly response from my friends who heard my job title for the first time, "Do you teach the gorillas?

"No," I'd say, tongue in cheek. "I teach baboons like you."

But it was clear that urban folks, like my friends, isolated in a world of concrete and glass, needed wildlife education.

If they knew nothing about the beauty of rapidly vanishing fauna, how could they contribute to its protection? As the naturalist William Beebe claimed, another harmony may yet inspire a composer of lost music and another Rembrandt may yet materialize, but a species once vanished will not return to this heaven on earth.

I took my job seriously—maybe some days even too seriously—and enjoyed working under a smart ecologist whose knowledge was prodigious and as striking as his shock of red hair. Like many of my zoo colleagues, Tom had come from the Midwest. It seemed like that part of the country—with its vast open prairies, woodlands, and forests—was the fertile breeding grounds of what zoo folks called "Animal People." In fact, according to an unwritten zoo employee classification scheme, there were only two types of *Homo sapiens*: animal people and everyone else. Animal people had a nearly innate gift for understanding animals and all their mysterious ways. They could identify species in the field, handle the most cantankerous animals with ease, and practically tell what the beasts were thinking. The rest of us, insensate blobs, could only study and learn about animals, yet never achieve that inborn sense of empathy. And perhaps that was true. Even after years of experience with the ways of the zoo, I thought the true "Animal People" would never include me in their ranks.

Tom could go on forever about bird songs and animal mutations and reptiles of every type. "Did you know that birds can control the two sides of their trachea independently to produce two notes at once?" He loved to toss out little-known, tantalizing tidbits of biology as he sipped his morning coffee and twirled his red mustache. "How about those horned desert lizards?" he'd say with a smile, and we'd be all ears. "Isn't is fantastic how they can shoot streams of blood out of their eyes to deter predators? Pretty cool, ha?" I think reptiles were his favorite. He spoke of lizards and turtles and snakes with such passion that anyone listening would be filled with curiosity. I always thought that if he ever had a child, the kid would know everything there was to know about animals. Tom and his young wife lived in a building located immediately behind the renowned Reptile House, famous for its huge pythons, anacondas, and crocodiles, a place that would be exhilarating to most children. Some days I imagined that living on the grounds of a magnificent park, in proximity to storied beasts must be rather exciting, even relaxing.

And then it happened. Tom's wife became pregnant, despite his apprehensions about adding to the human population on earth, since we are threatening to swallow all the wilderness. Despite his scientific persuasion, Tom became an enthusiastic father. He cruised the zoo paths after hours with the stroller, showing the animals to his little girl before she could even say, "Da-da." He'd sometimes invite staff to his home, and whenever I was there it struck me as odd that a pink baby nursery looked directly at the building that housed fear-provoking reptiles.

One evening, Tom and his wife hosted a picnic in their backyard, in back of the Reptile House. We feasted on barbecued ribs and sat in the little yard while Tom showed us the vegetable garden he'd planted. By now his little red-haired girl was nearly two, and I watched her as she toddled from guest to guest, gathering handfuls of soil and pebbles and offering them in her grimy little palm. I wondered what she would grow up to be, living so close to nature. A naturalist perhaps, comfortable handling frogs and toads? Or maybe she would work with something larger, like wild cats, or even poisonous snakes? By the time she was in elementary school she wouldn't need the kinds of classes I taught; she could teach them herself. My husband and I went home late and tired, but pleased by the camaraderie between the animal people and us ordinary mortals.

I came to work tired the next day, but sensed that something was wrong right away. Tom was nowhere to be seen, and he was usually first at the office. Small wonder, he didn't have far to travel. The secretary was on the phone arguing with someone trying to get through to Tom. My instructor colleagues were not there either. A moment later, one of them ran in with a panicked expression on her face. "What's going on?" I asked.

"Haven't you heard?" she shot back, "A king cobra is on the loose!"

It took me a few moments to absorb her statement. A venomous carnivore capable of killing an elephant with a single bite is out of its enclosure? I knew the Reptile House specimen was enormous. I didn't know its exact size, but I knew that king cobras could reach eighteen feet in length, although an average one would be around ten or eleven feet. Tom's child lived right next door. This was terrifying.

"Is it still in the building? What are the keepers saying?" I sputtered questions, thinking of the toddler.

"It may have gotten out of the building, they aren't sure yet," she replied. Goose bumps rose on my arms.

By now the secretary was off the phone. "Wait, it gets better," she said, as if relishing the opportunity to participate in such an exciting caper. "Tom's little girl was by herself in their yard when the keepers discovered the snake missing."

"Holy shit, how long had she been there by herself?" I blurted out. "What's being done?" I asked, and didn't wait for a reply. I left the office running toward Tom's house.

There was already a crowd of employees on the path leading toward the Reptile House. Fortunately, the zoo was not yet open to the public, but it would open soon. What if they didn't find the escaped snake by then? I felt agitated and asked about Tom. A keeper told me he was in his house as we spoke, searching high and low for the animal. Horror of horrors, I was so firmly focused on the previous night's image of the child in the garden, it hadn't occurred to me that the king cobra might slither into the house.

My mind filled with grizzly images: the little girl standing wide-eyed in front of the cobra, a third of its muscular body reared up, its hood flared and a frightening hissing sound bringing her to tears, then the screams of her mother discovering the mayhem. The possibilities were endless. Poor Tom and his wife, how would they go to bed if the animal wasn't found by the end of the day? Surely, they wouldn't leave the little one in her room alone. She was certainly different from the king cobra's usual meal of other snakes, but I imagined it might not turn down a meal of a small mammal. The situation seemed surreal and it struck me that Tom and his child may have indeed been better off if they lived in an enclosure, as my silly friends had joked. But this was no joking matter.

As a parent of young children myself, I was glad we didn't live on zoo grounds. Now I found myself pushing aside the romantic notions I sometimes harbored about how idyllic it would be to live in a place safely surrounded by gorillas, zebras, tigers, and yes, even anacondas, to go to sleep with the roar of the lions and dream that the wilderness would be there forever.

Shortly before the zoo was to open, the crowd of curious employee onlookers was dispersed by security. A frenetic search by a team of reptile keepers was on. The Reptile House remained closed while they scoured every corner, looked beneath large metal tubs, behind odd pieces of equipment and coils of rubber hoses, around glass terrariums, in boxes of hooks, tongs, and probes. I prayed that the fugitive would slither to the Bronx River—rivers in India and Southeast Asia harbor plenty of them— and bypass Tom's backyard.

The missing snake was nowhere to be found.

The Reptile House remained closed, but the zoo opened to the public as usual. The day wore on without any news. Tom stopped by the office briefly, looking so exhausted that no one dared to say anything. The mood of the staff was sober and the prospects were grim.

At the end of the workday, everyone went home dispirited. I simply could not picture Tom and his wife in their home with their child and the possibility that the king cobra was hiding somewhere in the rafters of that old building, waiting to come out when it sensed a tasty morsel. Maybe they should have gone to a nearby motel? No, the one near the zoo did mostly an hourly business. What about staying with friends? My sleep was filled with nightmares. When I woke up I was glad that I hadn't shared the story with my kids. I went to work hoping that daylight and a fresh search would be productive. Who knows, by now they may have already found it, I thought, trying to be optimistic.

Despite everyone's hopes, the snake did not materialize, not on that day, nor the second or the third. Like all fears, though, the sense of disquiet seemed to diminish with each passing day. After a while, it seemed as if it was quite ordinary to be missing a large venomous serpent, misplaced like a set of keys or reading glasses. Even Tom grew calmer as he gradually became accustomed to the notion that his child might one day come nose-to-nose with a very large pet. The mood grew lighter and I began to joke with Tom.

"What if she's playing in the yard one day and comes across it?" I asked jovially.

"Oh, she'll probably just think it's a very big worm," he said with a relaxed grin.

♦ ♦ ♦

Several days passed and it wasn't until everything seemed normal that the king cobra was discovered in a dark corner, behind the scenes in the Reptile House. The keepers spoke of the find with the nonchalance of experts. "We knew it would turn up one day." What a story the little girl would have to tell as she got older, I thought with relief when I heard the news.

Some time later Tom lost his job to a competitor. He and his family moved away from the zoo and I didn't see him for many years, but one day he stopped in when he was in town. We reminisced and I asked him if his daughter remembered anything of the king cobra incident.

"Nah," he said, "She has bigger problems related to her time at the zoo."

"What?" I asked, imagining her so traumatized by the frantic search in her old home that she was withdrawn, had no friends, or harbored deep-seated animal fears.

"Every time she moves to a new school and is asked where she was born, she says 'the zoo.' The teachers think she's being a smart alec."

"If they only knew," I said, laughing.

"And we never told her about the king cobra," he said. "Luckily she was too young to remember *that*."

CHAPTER 11

Growing Pains

One day I noticed a cluster of parents and kids in green T-shirts and shorts, clutching overstuffed duffels, waiting at a corner near my house. I overheard they were about to board a bus that would take them to a camp in the Catskills. The mothers looked anxious and pleaded with the children, "Remember Robbie, you promised to brush your teeth *every* night." "Joanne, do you know where I packed your bee sting kit?" Bingo! Immediately, an idea lodged in my brain: we should create a camp at the zoo! We could offer so much excitement and kids wouldn't have to schlep on a bus, making their mothers wracked with worry, I thought. It was the first summer after I started working at the zoo, and I had much yet to learn about breaking with tradition.

When I joined the Education staff only a small selection of programs was offered, mostly to elementary grade school children. The programs had cheesy titles like "Rats, Roaches, and their Cousin, the Possum." I had no idea what that one was all about, and I never did get a chance to observe it in action. Where was the excitement in the programs we offered? The imagination? I knew we could do better.

Once I understood the richness and diversity of the zoo's exhibitions and knew every inch of our magnificent park, I wanted to offer a wider variety of programs, not just for school classes but for individual children as well. And a camp would be just perfect. I was the only parent in the group at the time, and I was convinced that if we ran a summer camp where a city kid could fulfill a fantasy of spending more time at the zoo and even stay overnight, we'd be the most popular place to spend summers. After all, we had the resources: a wonderful collection of handleable animals, fascinating mammals, birds and reptiles on exhibit, lush woods, a meadow, a river, various animal rides, and knowledgeable instructors with a passion for sharing what they knew.

I headed out to the Administration building to discuss my zoo camp idea, bubbling with enthusiasm. I was sure the man responsible for approving such a venture would love the idea, maybe even wonder why no one had proposed it before. To my surprise, I was shot down like a goose decoy at a skeet range. Mr. J. sat there in his business suit, surrounded by stacks of reports, time sheets, and memos, completely unmoved by my excitement. "There must be good reasons why other zoos haven't done it," he said when I told him we'd be innovators. When I carefully explained my rationale, he still balked and threw out roadblocks so fast I was reeling. "We don't have a license to run a children's program; we have no full-time doctor on staff; never mind what having children in our care would do to our already high cost of insurance." Yikes! Insurance. I hadn't thought of that. No, no, no was all I heard then, and my camp idea became a big topic of discussion during the whole first year I was at the zoo.

I went home that first day deflated. I stewed and complained to David as he stood there in his apron preparing dinner… again. "Here I thought we could send our kids to zoo camp, silly me."

"Well, did you want it for our kids, or was it a bigger idea?" David asked.

"What's the matter with you? You know I'm trying to shake up those old timers! I've got to get them to see the possibilities." Now the kids, smelling dinner, showed up.

"Mom, mom, are we going to your zoo camp?" Jessica was jumping up and down.

"Not this year, honey. Sit down and eat."

"Oh, I thought you could try out that piñata game on us," she was crestfallen.

Jeremy also looked disappointed.

Their reaction only fueled my idea. I knew I'd need to dismantle the arguments *against* having a camp at the zoo, one by one. Over the next year, I dug in and spent a lot of time researching how we could obtain a license to operate a camp. First, I called the proper authorities at the Department of Health (not so easy to identify), then I read all the fine print in the regulations. It turned out that since we had no swimming pool and no intention of having campers swim with the sea lions, our licensing hurdles would be easier to overcome. Whew, what a relief. Except for what we might get from our accredited restaurant, we would not be preparing food and could provide refrigeration for children's lunches—so another problem was solved. Did our staff have the minimum requirements to serve as counselors? Of course, they did—most had advanced science degrees, so we far exceeded this requirement. But the insurance issue could prove to be insurmountable. I chewed up several pencils before an idea struck me: why don't we just ask our current carrier. And here I struck gold: it turned out our campers would be covered under the zoo's existing policy *at no additional cost.*

◆◆◆

I breathed a sigh of satisfaction when I received very cautious permission from the administration to run a small pilot camp program. And my own children were as thrilled as I was. They, along with their peers, would be our guinea pigs. Their reactions would tell me what programs and activities should be dropped or modified.

The department staff and I plunged into planning the camp activities. Everyone was excited with the prospect of doing something different. These children would really want to be here, and since their parents would be paying for the camp, we had to provide the best possible experience. No mind-numbing babysitting or coloring books!

We'd combine education with sheer fun. We would not only study birds, we would *show* kids the principles of flight.

They would make different models of paper planes, build fancy kites and have flying competitions, and dissect real owl pellets to reconstruct the prey they had eaten. We would illustrate the difference between raptors (like hawks) and seed-eaters (like doves) by bringing them face-to-face with the children in our classroom. We would take our campers into the Children's Zoo to become keepers for a day, letting them feed the animals and help clean their enclosures. We'd have scavenger hunts across the park, culminating in special behind-the-scenes animal demonstrations. The children would ride on animals like camels and elephants, the Skyfari gondola and the monorail, even golf carts. We would end every week with a magnificent piñata party for our little V.I.P.'s. And best of all, any child who wanted to stay in the zoo overnight after the week-long experience could do so in our overnight safari.

We planned the activities to the minutest detail for months, then put out a camp brochure and sat back to watch the response. It was overwhelming. By May, all of our July and August sessions were booked solid! The administration's concern that parents would not want to drive the children to and from the zoo each day from Westchester County, Manhattan, or other parts of the city proved to be as unfounded as the idea that wild-born tigers can be tamed, or that cats steal your breath.

◆ ◆ ◆

The program took off like a peregrine falcon. Our campers were mesmerized by the activities. We debriefed at the end of each day to tweak the routes through the park and adjust the timing of each activity, all in order to maximize the fun. But being a worrier by nature, I was concerned something could go wrong despite our meticulous planning. Sure enough, something happened on day three.

It was an Africa-themed day, and among the many activities we planned were camel rides. I didn't know that our camel manager had put a newly-trained camel to work on the track that day. The camel performed well all morning, and the keeper assigned to lead it around the track reported nothing unusual. Our campers came in the afternoon, and several children completed their ride around the track without incident, but then something went amiss.

The new camel may have been spooked by a noise, or perhaps it was just tired, though camels have great endurance and are commonly used as transportation on long trips in North Africa and the Middle East. Whatever the reason, when the next-to-last pair of campers were loaded onto the dromedary it took a few steps then balked, spit, and jumped, knocking the kids to the ground. It happened so quickly that neither the children nor the staff knew how to react. The little girl and boy were bruised on their elbows and knees, but so surprised they didn't even cry. The nurse was summoned immediately to provide first aid. I called the parents to tell them of the incident and to ask if they wanted us to take the children to a nearby hospital to have them checked out. As fate would have it, both parents were physicians! Now, I've done it, I thought. Mr. J. would fire me. This was exactly what he had been worried about. The parents spoke with our nurse and determined that there was no need for a hospital visit.

Since such accidents were extremely rare, the staff and administration buzzed about it for hours, then days. Rumors flew. We'd be sued. We'd lose our license. Camel rides would be toast. Our insurance would skyrocket. And worst of all, the zoo camp would have to close. Luckily, despite our litigious society, reason prevailed. There were no frightful consequences and the two children who fell returned and even took part in the sleepover, which would become an instant sensation, like the Beatles.

I was thrilled that we could make every child's dream of remaining at the zoo after all visitors were gone a reality. After a cookout with s'mores, ice cream, and animal stories, the campers embarked on a flashlight safari once it was completely dark. For many of them, this was the most anticipated part of the camp. They would prowl the zoo grounds to see as many animal eyes as possible, equipped only with their curiosity and the small flashlights we provided. "Will it be scary?" some of the younger campers asked when we explained the nocturnal trek.

"It might be, but it'll be exciting and the group that spots the most eyes will win a special prize," was our response.

For any child who was frightened or even a little bit worried, we offered to call their parents so they could go home, but no one ever took us up on that offer. We assured them all that after the flashlight safari they would be back safely to watch special movies with popcorn and then snuggle in their sleeping bags with their favorite stuffed animals.

My staff and I anticipated the first overnight safari with almost as much excitement as the campers. I wanted it all to be perfect, with no slip-ups or mishaps, like bridezilla anticipating her wedding day. But I knew that the week before our first overnight, there had been an animal escape. Maybe that was the reason for my anxiety. Fortunately, that escape took place just *after* public hours. There were a fair number of keepers on the grounds because they were celebrating a colleague's retirement, and as they partied on the lawn just outside the zoo's cafeteria, suddenly someone called out: "A bear is loose!" For a moment, it seemed like a party prank stimulated by an excess of beer.

And it was not just any bear, though a black bear weighing in at 400 pounds would be bad enough. This was a male Kodiak bear weighing over 1,000 pounds and at least ten feet tall standing on its hind legs. Our male Kodiak bear shattered a heretofore-unbreakable glass window and decided to take a stroll on zoo grounds that beautiful June night. The curator of birds found the bear (not his cup of tea) around 7:30 p.m. The bear had wandered down the steps to Beaver Valley and strolled along to the World of Birds. He then lumbered up the ramp to the upper level and looked down at the keepers, who had arrived to deal with the situation, before coming down to where he was tranquillized. By 8:30 p.m., he was back in the holding area where a vasectomy was performed so he never had to be separated from the females again and walk out in protest. It was a miracle that several mammal experts were on hand and knew just how to handle the dangerous situation.

But the knowledge that such an escape was possible gnawed at me. I knew it was extremely unlikely to happen again, especially now that special precautions were instituted after a thorough analysis of how the escape happened in the first place. But still… human error—forgetting to lock a cage— was bound to happen again in the future. I was responsible for other people's children, and the notion that it happened once gave me pause. Before the overnight session, I gathered my staff and we reviewed the safety procedures. Fully-charged radios tuned to the security channel? Check. Lists of phone numbers: parents, nurse, hospital, nearest police precinct? Check. First aid kits? "Hey boss, you didn't think we'd forget those?" one of the youngest assistants piped up. The tension was broken and we all had a good laugh.

As the park emptied of visitors and a blissful quiet descended, our overnight campers launched joyfully into the planned activities. They admired the barn owl and screech owl demonstration as they learned about special nocturnal adaptations. They dissected owl pellets and reassembled tiny rodent skeletons, the owl's past dinner. They devoured hamburgers, hot dogs and ice cream, and after setting up for the night they were finally ready for the grand finale —the flashlight safari.

Split up into small groups of ten campers, they set out, ready to explore. Would they spot the eyes of the lions on African Plains? The deer? The cheetahs? The owls in the Birds of Prey Aviary? It depended on the path they chose and how good they were as observers. The children tiptoed close together, following their group leaders. They were a little apprehensive, having never heard the zoo's night sounds, but they were very excited. In some areas of the zoo grounds they might not see much, but they could hear a virtual orchestra of creatures: the chirping trills of American toads, low-pitched sounds of the spadefoots, bell-like calls of the peepers, owl hoots, the cackles of the night herons and wolf howls. The whole place was alive with nature's sounds, only occasionally interrupted by a distant siren. Stars twinkled in a velvet sky. It was pure magic in the heart of the most urban metropolis on the planet.

Suddenly, there was a rustling sound in the bushes. "Shh . . ." The instructor stopped with a line of children behind her grasping each other's hands more tightly.

"Don't worry, it might be a squirrel or a raccoon."

But the noise came closer, now accompanied by an ominous growl. Were it lighter, the children would have seen their group leader's face go white. She shushed the children again, though there was no need, they were as quiet as mute swans. The growling became louder and louder, and a figure seemed to be lurking and shuffling nearby, hidden in the vegetation. Then, without warning, it burst out of the bushes. It was large and stooped and began moving slowly, deliberately toward the group. The dark made it impossible to discern exactly what it was.

In the pitch dark, it took the poor counselor a few moments to discern the identity of the bear-like form. It was none other than... my boss. He began to laugh his deep belly laugh. "Did I scare you?" he asked.

"Well... I... I... I thought it may have been the bear again," she replied, her teeth still chattering. The kids, having realized it was a joke began to giggle first, then laugh.

When I recovered from the shock of hearing the story, I knew that if anyone were to play a prank like that it would have been him. When he stashed a fish in one employee's drawer several months before, it should have been a hint. In the morning, the kids in this group had some story to tell: we ran into a bear on our safari, they boasted. When their peers refused to believe it, the counselor confirmed the claim.

What a tale they'd have for their school friends!

I sat at my desk and popped a leftover s'more in my mouth, already planning next summer's camp.

CHAPTER 12

Natural Affinity

My work kept me nearly chained to my desk, so taking a short walk around the lushly landscaped 265-acre park was a rare treat. For the most part, I tried to make my walks utilitarian: going to a meeting in another part of the campus, checking out a new exhibit for creative interpretive opportunities, or observing instructors conducting one of the courses I oversaw. But on that October day, I took a walk for the sheer pleasure of the brilliant weather. I also needed to clear my head after a contentious meeting in which one of the curators had insisted on a dogmatic interpretation of animal behavior. I was representing the Education Division's point of view on a planned Congo Forest exhibition. During a spirited discussion about the text that would eventually appear on one of the signs, I had raised a question: Did herbivores ever eat anything other than plants?

"Herbivores would never touch anything other than vegetable matter," the curator had said combatively, as if I had questioned his very reason for existence.

"Never?" I asked.

He looked angry and his face turned red.

"We are talking about scientific principles here," he said with a finality that made it clear the discussion was over.

"Okay, Okay, take it easy," I said, "I was just curious if there could be any variation."

He turned to someone else and refused to engage with me any further.

Fine, I thought, but wished he had more curiosity. Animal curators seemed to be very driven by their particular specialty—mammologists didn't seem to care much about reptiles; nor ornithologists about mammals, and the herpetologists were in a world of their own. They were all intensely focused on how to best care for and breed the species in their charge. Educators like me spent their lives thinking about how to transmit respect for animals and an understanding of their ecology. Sometimes it felt as if we lived on different planets. The meeting lasted longer than it should have, as they often did. I decided that a nice walk would clear my head of all the cigarette smoke in the room.

It was well past three o'clock, but I had skipped lunch and allowed myself this bit of luxury. After all, working in a place that was an urban oasis for others should allow me a chance to indulge in its beauty. A light breeze swirled the orange leaves and with each gust more came down off the old oaks. Autumnal colors rained from the trees and the crunching underfoot was a reminder of childhood days spent hiding in stacks of dry, rustling piles in the park.

A pungent whiff told me I was approaching the elephant house where hulking gray bodies were massed in front of the building's door, anxious to go inside. It must be close to their feeding time, I thought. Then I walked down a path that was rarely filled with visitors. It meandered around the Mouse House, whose interesting assortment of small furry creatures—kangaroo rats, flying squirrels, chinchillas—was old fashioned and generally ignored by visitors more interested in modern exhibitions.

The path led toward the giraffe enclosure. I've always loved those tall, elegant giants. They seemed to me like Italian women strutting in their finery along Via Montenapoleone in their Manolo Blahniks. Their very bearing was regal. The way they towered over other species and could reach as tall as twenty feet high was nothing short of remarkable. I was still quite a distance from the exhibit when I caught sight of something preposterous. No, it can't be, I said to myself. I adjusted my glasses, making sure it wasn't a trick of my vision. The tallest giraffe in the distance seemed to have a long droopy, gray mustache.

The strangeness of the image made my mind swirl over rocks and eddies. What had happened to this stunning beauty? Hair hanging off her lips? Did she miss a waxing? No, it couldn't be. I moved closer and tilted my short neck up, my eyes aimed thirteen feet above me, my mouth opened. I'd have exclaimed, but I didn't want to frighten the animal, or any visitors who may have come by.

The giraffe had a pigeon in its mouth, whose wings drooped limply on either side. The sight was so extraordinary that it didn't occur to me right away that what I was witnessing contradicted the obstinate curator's statements, not a half-hour before. I stood with my mouth open, waiting to see what would happen next, while my mind churned with theories.

Did this elegant lady move her head too close to the tree nearby and inadvertently sweep the hapless bird into her mouth, upsetting its afternoon rest? With that graceful, flexible neck, it was possible. Had she tired of her daily rations of alfalfa hay and dry pellets and decided to quit her vegan diet? Was she perhaps remembering her childhood days on the savannah and how she admired the nimble moves of the cheetah to catch her meaty meal? Was she craving a more varied diet with more protein? Did she simply decide to be brave and rebel, be a leader and leave her shorter sisters in the dust? I don't know how many minutes passed, because I was so absorbed in my speculations and flights of fancy. Then I saw her begin to munch on the bird. She chewed slowly, much as one would tasting an unfamiliar dish. She reminded me of when I tried to chew a sea cucumber the first time I tasted it in a Chinese restaurant—slow, cautious mastication, as if to delay the actual act of swallowing. A few more minutes and the bird disappeared, the gray mustache was gone. In the absence of a linen napkin, she flicked out her foot-and-half-long tongue and wiped her lips clean of the squab *crudo* meal.

After that, I lingered in front of the exhibition and looked up into her gentle eyes with lashes to rival Elizabeth Taylor's. My curiosity intensified, and I wondered what she experienced. My imagination was stoked. Did she close her eyes and dream of roaming in the continent below the equator? Did she remember how a Nile crocodile dragged her baby sister under while she was getting a drink? "Who's to say giraffes don't dream?" I mumbled to myself.

Mesmerized by their graceful gait, I watched three other giraffes who shared this beauty's enclosure before moving on. They were strutting slowly, their languid movements constrained by the exhibit space, but I thought about their wild sisters on the beige, undulating stretches of the African grassland. I knew they could move at great speeds, in an easy 35 mile-per-hour trot. They were so different from us and yet so similar, with their seven-boned neck, just like ours, and uniquely patterned skin, like our fingerprints. I also admired this giraffe's adventurous spirit.

Had I just witnessed evolution in action? A divine accident or a mishap, an unintended collision of two species? I will never know the answer, but I learned to always be wary of rigid answers, whether science or any other area of human inquiry provides them. The observation suited me, a born skeptic.

As I moved away, I imagined a dialogue with the giraffe. "Thank you for showing me that even animals can break out of a routine and take chances," I'd say.

"It's nothing," she'd reply, "but pigeon is hardly haute cuisine."

◆ ◆ ◆

Watching people at the zoo was sometimes even more interesting than observing the animals. Something curious happens when people look at animals. It's as if they are looking at a magic mirror, and seeing the animals' unusual or embarrassing behaviors instead of their own. They can ogle the animal without any sense of discomfort, something that would be unimaginable if they were watching another person. They can laugh with impunity when an ape does something that reminds them of Uncle Hal at Thanksgiving, and no one around them is the wiser.

Of course, anthropomorphic conclusions about animal behaviors are almost always wrong. Baboons don't yawn, exposing their impressive teeth, because they are tired, and monkeys don't avoid direct eye contact because they are shy. We are apt to misread animal behaviors, but to most visitors that hardly matters. What does matter is that people have had an insatiable interest in animals dating to prehistory. The caves at Lascaux in Southwestern France bear evidence that more than seventeen thousand years ago, humans were observing animals and recording what they saw faithfully in paintings on the walls. And it's no surprise that children's fables are chock-full of creatures with human-like traits: cunning foxes, naïve pigs, sophisticated mice, and champion turtles—a diverse bestiary of creatures. Even the Old Testament and the Qur'an instruct followers to respect animals.

Among the most interesting animal observers at the Bronx Zoo were students who played hooky from school and stole past the gate guards. For a time, the zoo employed full-time truant officers to find these rule-breakers and return them to their classrooms, but to these kids the zoo proved to be the best kind of school. They'd often be caught unawares by the officer because they were standing totally absorbed and mesmerized by the big cats, the monkeys, or the reptiles. Being returned to face an angry principal was not the biggest punishment—missing out on seeing the animals that made their imaginations soar was far worse. To these students, the creatures may have possessed imagined powers they could share. Some of these rule-breakers were repeat offenders, willing to risk stiffer punishments just to see the pythons devouring chickens once more, the tigers snarling, or the peacocks who had also escaped from their enclosures, strutting around as if they owned the place.

While most of the exhibit observers were children who shouted with excitement at every move of the animal on view and then moved on to the next one after a mere two or three minutes, we also had a steady following of adults. These dedicated animal-watchers would plant themselves in front of an exhibit, whether of elephants, sea lions, or cheetahs, and sit spellbound for long periods of time. I enjoyed watching them looking at the animals and I attempted to guess what motivated them to devote such large chunks of time to this silent contemplation.

The preoccupation of some was easy to understand. Often, I saw them snapping away, taking countless photos with their cameras, long telephoto lenses at the ready, along with fancy flash units or expensive tripods. Some sat patiently with sketchpads, waiting for the animal to change its pose so they could render it with more accuracy. But others were more difficult to figure out. They just sat there motionless and followed the animal with their eyes, ignoring the rumpus around them. I often wondered if they looked at the animals seeking inspiration for their poetry or children's stories, or if they were gathering data for a research project. No matter the reason for such concentrated attention, I was happy to see them silently interacting with the animals, because I knew they would be our allies in protecting the natural world.

A small number of zoo regulars didn't fit into any of these categories. They operated on a different plane. One elderly man, gaunt and rarely shaven, stood in his perennial beige raincoat and waved an open black umbrella over the sea lion pool. When we'd ask him what he was doing he'd say, "I'm cleaning the pollution out of the air. Pollution is not good for them." He was on duty every spring.

Not to be outdone was a middle-aged woman who used to clamber up the steps to our offices in the Heads and Horns building with her bulky stroller. She'd come huffing and puffing to the front desk and ask the clerk if there was any place she could wash her children's hands. "You know how they love to come to the zoo," she'd say, "but they get their hands dirty every time." The first time the clerk looked over her counter into the stroller she nearly exclaimed in shock—the children were a row of cabbage patch dolls. This woman must have found some solace in watching the animals with her "children" because she, too, was a regular.

But of all the unusual instances of humans communing with animals, the most remarkable one I saw took place around the Jewish holiday of Succoth on an October afternoon. During days two through seven of this week-long harvest festival, Jews celebrate the bounty of nature. On these days, they follow religious practice, but are encouraged to relax and take family outings. On that day, I observed large family groups dressed in festive outfits, crisp white shirts for the boys, long-sleeved dresses and knee socks for the girls.

These Hassidic families strolled through the zoo with as many as a dozen children in tow. From their clothing I could see they belonged to this strictly observant Jewish sect. The men wore wide-brimmed black hats, shiny black frocks and white stockings, and the women wore long skirts and wigs under their headscarves. It was a lovely sight to observe them mixing with the other visitors, many of them black and Hispanic families: so many shades of skin, clothing styles, and languages. The zoo looked like a harmonious multi-ethnic melting pot, a sight rarely seen in other venues.

By early afternoon, most of the groups had gone. I happened to approach the Birds of Prey Aviary where I encountered a sight I'll never forget. From the distance, it looked vaguely as if a zebra, or more accurately an okapi had gotten out of its enclosure. All I could see were black and white stripes. As I got closer, I saw that it was a bearded Hassidic man, standing alone in front of the owl exhibit. His white beard nearly reached his chest, and a striped prayer shawl covered his shoulders.

The prayer book in his hands was open, so I hesitated on the path because I didn't want to disturb him. He looked intently at the snowy owl and it seemed to be looking right at him. The bird gave the impression of an otherworldly apparition in its blindingly white plumage. Its yellow eyes were fixed attentively on the man. What were they both thinking? After a few minutes, the man began to intone his prayers and swayed rhythmically, bending from his waist and bobbing up again and again. It was clear that this was an intensely personal and meaningful moment for him. I wondered what the nature of the prayer was. Perhaps he was communing with the animals, as Job instructs: "*But ask the beasts and they will teach you; the birds of the sky, they will tell you, or speak to the earth, it will teach you; the fish of the sea, they will inform you.*"

The following week, I came across two women and three children standing in front of the very same exhibit. The small women wore flowing peach-colored saris with gold and green threads. Despite the children's urgency to move on, the women looked at the owl with the same reverence as the Hassidic man. The small children pulled on the women's hands and whined, "Let's go." But the women stood there, unperturbed, as if trying to divine whose soul now occupied the white being in front of them.

CHAPTER 13

Not Much like a Platypus

There was no ignoring it: the noise on Astor Court outside my office was deafening. I walked outside to take in the scene, and was immediately reminded of why I needed to be doing the work I had chosen. Groups of students jockeyed for positions in front of the exhibits. Teachers called out instructions to their charges, and mothers with strollers struggled to push through the crowds, zigzagging amid the turmoil on their way to the Children's Zoo.

The spring season was in full swing, with its irresistible cacophony of sounds and colors. By late April, the zoo always pulsated with life: delicate leaves were unfurling, trees were shedding clouds of yellow pollen, and passing warblers, vireos, and wrens announced their presence with chirps and whistles. Canada geese honked and lounged everywhere, leaving abundant trails of green poop as they meandered on the elegant neoclassical court—the zoo's historic center.

Kids tried to shoo the honkers away, yelling "Out of the way, ducks!"

Ducks! Hadn't they ever read *Make Way for Ducklings?* On second thought, I considered, probably not. Too many of the inner-city children who visited had little exposure to books. They really do need this experience, I thought, and hoped that someone would clue them in. The children's puffy winter jackets hung loosely off their shoulders unzipped, scarves hung limply out of pockets, dragging on the ground. Shedding the winter this way was a New York tradition. And there were few places in the city more suited for such an exuberant spring transformation.

One of the great pleasures—and frustrations—of my job was working with teachers. Over the years, I had come across teachers who were struggling in under-resourced schools where the ceilings leaked and personal safety was an ever-present concern. They cared as deeply about their students as if they were their own children, and put in countless hours to create a warm learning atmosphere in their classrooms. Sadly, in some of the city's public schools these teachers were more the exception than the rule. And of all the subjects, science was nearly always the stepchild. That bothered me to no end, because I knew that if these children could excel in the sciences they'd have a greater chance of success in life, higher paying jobs would be open to them, taking them out of poverty. And even if they did not pursue science as a career, it would give them an underpinning of logic and a way to understand themselves and the world.

It didn't take more than a few minutes outside my Heads and Horns building to find proof that my division's task would never be done. As I approached the sea lion pool, the undisputed domain of a huge male named Moose, I heard a young teacher calling to her class, "Hey, kids, look at these seals. Aren't they cute?" *Cute?* When the 700-pound Moose opened his mouth, let out a loud bark and showed his canines, he looked anything but cute. He was formidable.

A short boy in glasses stood at the back of his group and mumbled, "They aren't seals," but she didn't hear him and he was too timid to press the point. Had the teacher prepared herself for the visit, she'd have known that sea lions have external ears, like the animals in front of her, while true seals lack them. Had she thought of the zoo trip as a science lesson, she could have informed her students that although both seals and sea lions are *pinnipeds* (fin-footed), sea lions spend more time on land and rocks with their elongated flippers, and are more social than seals. The teacher could even have *pretended* she had prepared, since the graphic panels directly in front of her said all of this and more.

I wondered if she'd have confused the Civil War and the Revolutionary War, after all they both involved combat and took place in America. I realized that my reaction to this teacher was harsh, and recalled my early days as a substitute teacher, years before, when I was clueless. Teaching could be stressful and financially unrewarding, yet I had seen other teachers with their students on zoo visits who were respectful and informed. Nothing was more dispiriting than the occasional teacher who was a mere babysitter, and not a good one at that.

While many zoos provided tours and programs of various types for school children, I felt this was a well-meaning but mostly ill-conceived strategy. If we wanted to influence the greatest number of young people to understand the life sciences and value the natural world, targeting school kids was not the best approach.

Most zoos are non-profit institutions, always struggling to raise more money for their operations. Even in the best facilities, the funds available for education programs are limited. The number of instructors and well-trained volunteer guides will never be sufficient to reach all the school children in each area. But my team and I hit on a concept that could affect infinitely more children: teaching the teachers, who, in turn, would pass on what they learned to their peers and students. After all, teachers spend 180 days a year with their students. And it was teachers like the one at the sea lion pool that gave me the idea.

The first challenge was to actually get the teachers to come, at least somewhat willingly, to our training programs. Most adults think zoos are for kids, and teachers are the biggest culprits of all. Oh, they'd have no problem attending with a class of unruly school kids in tow, but alone, they'd not be caught dead coming in advance of a zoo trip to prepare. Prepare? Teachers have enough on their plates as far as they are concerned. Too many think of zoo trips as a day off.

I spent enough years at the zoo overhearing teachers instruct their middle school students, "Meet me here at 12:30. Don't be late, the bus won't wait for you." Then they'd head off to the cafeteria for coffee with colleagues who had similarly dispatched their kids to do zoo "research." In our quest to fix this situation, we hit upon an idea: provide training workshops after school hours, and reward participating teachers with credit that counted toward badly-needed salary raises. They'd attend zoo school, get to see the animals up close, and be provided with the instructional tools to change a random field trip into a first-class science lesson.

We announced our first round of teacher courses with trepidation, but I was hopeful that it would work. After all, I'd been through this before. After the first year's mishaps, zoo camp had become one of our most popular programs, with yearly pressure for us to increase enrollment. The New York City Department of Health was so impressed with our meticulous program and safety planning that they invited us to conduct training for staff from other city day camps. And year after year, zoos around the country and all over the world emulated our camp program. It spread like wildfire, not only to zoos but also to museums and other institutions of informal learning, giving thousands of children something to remember for a lifetime. We just needed to have the same kind of success with teachers, I figured.

Who knew? Maybe in time we could even develop a master's level program in Conservation Life Science teaching. With so many institutions of higher education in the city, I was sure we could find a university partner. But first things first.

In no time at all we filled our first accredited workshop to capacity. Thirty elementary grade teachers showed up, and after introductions, we warmed them up by doing a simple observation exercise. The idea was that every scientist must be, first and foremost, a careful observer.

We instructed the teachers to form two rows, facing one another, and said, "Look very carefully at the person in front of you, then turn around." Then we asked everyone to change one small thing about their appearance: move a pin to a different spot, remove an earring, tuck in the shirt, and so on. Then they turned to face one another again to see if they could detect the change. More than half failed, and the point was made in good fun.

The program then focused on turning free-for-all zoo trips into real science lessons by finding links to the core curriculum: analyzing the protein content of zoo animal diets and comparing them to human nutritional needs; looking at how the seasons affect bird migrations; or observing what young monkeys learn from their parents. When it was time to wrap up the two hours, the teachers said, "But, we've just begun!" I pointed to the clock and knew they were hooked.

"Okay," I said, "Let's talk for a few minutes about any animals you keep in your classrooms. Raise your hand if you have any animals back at school."

Many hands shot up. I was both pleased and worried. Did they have enough information to care for these animals properly? Would they know how to take advantage of the teachable moments their animals present? "Tell you what," I said, "We will focus on this topic in the next class, but if anyone has an urgent question related to animal care, we can take a couple."

A small young woman with flowing black hair raised her hand first, with some urgency, so I called on her. She hesitated for a moment before blurting out, "My guinea pig laid an egg. What do I do now?" Was she pulling my leg? She looked dead serious. Low titters filled the room and her cheeks reddened.

"Umm... are you sure?" I asked cautiously, not wanting to offend her.

"Yes, I'm sure. There's a small, white egg in its cage." Holy cow, I thought, someone must have played a prank on this poor woman.

"You know that a guinea pig is a mammal, right?"

"I guess so," she said timidly.

"And you know that mammals bear live young?"

"Well... I think so, but what about that, you know, uh... oh... I can't think of its name."

"Oh, you mean the platypus, do you?"

"Yes, yes," she said excitedly. I was semi-relieved. At least she knew the only exception to the mammalian rule. Then someone yelled out, "The egg was a joke by one of your smart-alec kids." Momentarily, she looked stricken, but she swallowed her embarrassment and began to laugh. The class joined her, and so did I. When the laughter subsided, she said, "Boy, oh boy, do I need this course." And right there I knew that she would not be one of those teachers who mixed up seals with sea lions, bison with buffalo, or pigs with guinea pigs. Her courage to speak up and her openness to learning inspired me. After all, there were wonderful teachers in city schools if one knew how to find them and nurture them, and gave them the right tools and support.

She approached me sheepishly after class to apologize for her blunder. "Don't worry, we all make mistakes," I said, "What really counts is that you are trying to do something special for your students. Keeping a live animal in class is a challenge."

"Yes, they turn the heat off on the weekends so kids take turns taking Rosie, the guinea pig, home. But one student's Peruvian parents wanted to cook it." I didn't know how to respond. I knew that in her school, the student population consisted mostly of South American immigrants.

"Well, in this course we are all guinea pigs, of sorts, aren't we?" I asked.

"For sure," she said.

I looked around the classroom as the teachers gathered their belongings, preparing to go home. They chatted about the workshop excitedly and I knew they'd become our allies.

CHAPTER 14

Phantom Pandas

"You have been chosen to lead our trip to China," my boss told me with the gravity reserved for such a momentous announcement. I stared at him blankly for a moment before his words registered.

"But... but why me?" I asked. I could think of several more qualified leaders who should have been given this privilege.

"Well, weren't you born forty miles from the Chinese border?" His voice boomed and a barrage of his signature belly laughs filled the office.

"But I've never been to China," I said, then stopped, lest he think I didn't want to do it. Inside, I was nervous, but overjoyed. China! How else would I ever afford to get there?

After all, in 1983, I was still a mid-level educator pushing to break new ground in the way zoological collections could reach people. My head was full of ideas on how to make the excitement of a zoo visit transfer to the actual classroom, so that school science lessons could be as enjoyable as the outdoor visits students loved so much. Personal travel—vacation trips like hiking in the Monteverde Cloud Forest in Costa Rica listening to the calls of howler monkeys, or exploring the Galapagos islands in Ecuador, where harems of sea lions laze on pristine beaches —were only a hazy fantasy.

In the mid-seventies the zoo embarked on a travel program for its members, but leadership of those trips was strictly reserved for animal curators on the rise. A lowly educator like myself would not even dream of being recruited for such an assignment. But suddenly, it was happening. I snapped back to reality, to my boss delivering the details.

"Don't worry. Our travel agent is an experienced China hand. He'll set you and your group up and take care of all the visa logistics," my boss assured me, smiling like a fox.

It wasn't until later that it became clear why this juicy assignment went to me. In 1983, travel by Americans to China was still in its infancy, though our scientific and curatorial staff had traveled there before. Richard Nixon persuaded the Chinese to open the doors in the late seventies, but any notion of how to cater to foreign tourists was still sorely lacking. Moreover, I would not be leading an ordinary group of zoo members. I would be guiding a group of trustees and high-level donors from zoological gardens throughout the U.S. This would be a discerning and super-demanding group of individuals who had traveled far more extensively than I had. It would be up to me to cater to their whims, arbitrate disagreements, solve any problems that were sure to crop up, and even entertain them. A painful realization dawned on me: this is why none of the animal curators had wanted to lead this group. I would have to be den mother to the glitterati! I had to do something to make myself feel better about this trip, so I decided to recruit my Dad, an enthusiastic traveler, to join me. His calm presence would be reassuring. He had a knack for getting along with everyone, from the tax man to the police officer writing a ticket, and knew how to maintain peace at Thanksgiving dinners with guests expressing radically different political opinions. He accepted my invitation instantly.

◆ ◆ ◆

After many months of study about China's wildlife (the neglect of many species and their consumption by humans), its environmental and cultural issues, ethnic groups, politics, and even a small taste of Mandarin, I felt ready. Protracted behind-the-scenes negotiations with the Chinese authorities yielded a special government permit for us to enter the panda reserve in the Sichuan province. This was to be the highlight of the trip—seeing the shy secretive pandas in their natural digs, cavorting and stuffing themselves with bamboo, their dietary staple. When the permit was granted, we rejoiced. It was rare for any foreign group to be allowed to enter this restricted area, but one of our foremost scientists, Dr. George Schaller, had been assisting the Chinese with panda reproductive strategies, and they could not refuse him. As for panda exhibitions in zoos, the issue was a hot potato in the eighties and thereafter. Every zoo knew that pandas bring in crowds and fill the coffers, but it was the opinion of Dr. Schaller—the most trusted voice on the species— that rent-a-panda programs would deplete the critical numbers of pandas left in the wild. Despite this, New York Mayor Koch would wangle a pair of pandas—Ling Ling and Yun Yun—for a six-month loan at the Bronx Zoo the following year, a project unknown to me at the time of the China trip.

My group of travelers received ample briefings by mail and telephone: be flexible and accepting of unanticipated schedule changes, be curious about an unfamiliar culture, and refrain from smoking on the minibus. Everyone seemed to understand the ground rules, and no one raised objections. Soon enough, I waited anxiously at JFK airport to collect my thirteen charges. Most were arriving from cities throughout the U.S. As the flights arrived I met each of them and introduced myself. Their sophisticated facades melted away quickly. Nearly all expressed some variant of, "I can't wait to see the pandas." Their enthusiasm was evident in their comments.

"I managed to get a map of the Wolong reserve," one said.

"Do you think we will see the golden monkeys or the white-lipped deer?" another asked. And on and on it went.

It was time to board our fourteen-hour fight to Narita airport in Japan, where we would stop briefly, then continue to Beijing. The only problem was that one woman was still missing. She did not contact me, and I had no way to reach her. I uttered a silent profanity. Did her absence augur trouble? I could not jeopardize twelve tickets. We got on the flight without her. My stomach churned. How should I handle one lost group member this early in the game?

Somehow the missing woman, a slightly hunched brunette in her sixties, made her way to Narita on her own. When she located me, she revealed sheepishly that her luggage had been lost. As if that wasn't bad enough, she had packed her prescription medications in her suitcase and her cameras as well. "I am not continuing to China without them," she announced imperiously, and told me, "I'll have you know, young lady, that I'm a medical doctor." A doctor! Even I knew that medication belonged in your carry-on—what was she thinking?

Our group's next departure was delayed untill the following morning. I parked my twelve travelers at the airport hotel while I scrambled to have the doctor's medications replaced. Dad gave me a knowing wink, and I was glad someone understood my frustration. But the missing medications were the least of it. She insisted on purchasing replacement cameras. That meant a train trip with her into Tokyo, which after the long flight strained every muscle and nerve in my body. I worried that we'd board the wrong train or I'd lose her again in the massive crowds. The city was completely alien to both of us. It was a major challenge locating the store the hotel clerk had scribbled on a note, and I was ill-prepared to answer her endless questions about camera equipment. This does not bode well, I groaned, as I crashed in my tiny airport hotel room to plan the next day's activities. If I were a drinker, I'd have ordered a stiff one to calm my nerves, but that wasn't me.

The bleary-eyed group waited for me at the departure lounge at six in the morning. I thought we were ready to go through security, but the late-arriving doctor was, once again, nowhere to be seen. I kept glancing at my watch as the others looked at me expectantly. Cutting it much too close, she finally ambled down the ramp, fussing with her oversized purse, tickets, and two new cameras dangling from her neck.

Her appearance signaled the group to move on. Eager to board the plane, they rushed through security and scattered down a long hallway. I followed them quickly, so as not to lose my brood. Though most were at least two decades older than me, I had come to think of them as my chicks. I still hadn't memorized all their faces. Would I be able to spot them among the other travelers?

At last I recognized my people huddled in front of the gate. I smiled with relief and collected their passports and tickets—just as I'd been instructed by the tour operator to do— then I took a count. Twelve? The friggin' doctor was missing. I swallowed my frustration and said in my most friendly professional tone, "Stay right here folks, I'll be right back." I ran, breathless, encumbered by my heavy backpack, bulging purse, and all the tickets and passports, all the way down an endless corridor back to the security gate.

I recognized her raspy bark immediately. Her loud argument with armed guards could be heard at a distance.

"I'm the group leader," I announced, trying to appear simultaneously authoritative and cooperative. "Can you tell me what the problem is?" I addressed a guard who seemed to be in charge, but his English was minimal. After a lot of hand gesturing, I understood that she had set off the alarm repeatedly. "Sir, our flight is boarding right now, please," I pleaded, although I couldn't know what potentially banned, illicit substance had caused the ruckus.

I pulled her aside and said, as gently as I could although I wanted to scream, "Doctor, you'll miss the plane again and so will the entire group. What is going on?"

"If you must know, I wear a metal body brace," she said with a mixture of defiance and pride.

Holy Jesus! I was baffled. Why hadn't she disclosed this on the medical forms? I would have been prepared to shepherd her through security first. Luckily, I spotted a female guard and asked her to do a pat down for the doctor who submitted, glaring at me. We ran to the gate, but this time I dragged her overstuffed bag along with all of my other belongings, and good thing, because we would've missed the flight if I hadn't.

I calmed down when we were aloft and thought how lucky I was that my dad had agreed to accompany me on this trip. At seventy-five he was still in good shape and an avid explorer. His calm, easy-going demeanor was a salve to my frayed nerves. "Don't worry, Ania," he said, "all inconveniences will be forgotten when we get to the panda reserve. These folks can't wait to get there."

◆◆◆

Our first impression of Beijing, after a thankfully uneventful flight, was out the plane window on landing: fields and fields lined the sides of the runways and stretched as far as the eye could see. "They have a billion people to feed here," Dad remarked. "They have to utilize every inch of space."

We entered the great arrivals hall, which reverberated with the sound of our footsteps. Except for us and well over a dozen military personnel, no one was there; it was like a mausoleum. The stiff stances and stony faces of the military men were accompanied by rifles held stiffly at their shoulders. Their eyes followed our every step. No arrival in a new country had been so fraught for me. Soon, the designated Chinese guide and a Communist party functionary met and escorted us to the hotel in a minibus, where the doctor promptly lit up her cigarette to the groans of the group.

The hotel was a sprawling six-story modern building made of prefabricated concrete in the staid, perfectly symmetrical Soviet style. Next to it a taller hotel was under construction, although the sight of a horse hitched to wagons hauling stacks of bricks to the site was jarring, almost comical and surreal. A high-rise hotel, built with the aid of horses! Obviously, I hadn't yet understood China's Great Leap Forward. But it became clearer after dinner when we were invited to visit the hotel's huge gift shop—selling souvenirs to visitors had just become a thing. Like the airport, the store was empty and so dim it was difficult to see the merchandise in the glass display cases. At my father's suggestion, I returned to my room to get my flashlight. "And bring the tape recorder too," he suggested, "I bet they've never seen such a device."

I could hardly believe the reaction when I brought both down. The sales girls, about a dozen of them, all young with peaches-and-cream complexions, wearing colorful, embroidered silk cheongsam-style dresses in blues and pinks, crowded around and looked at the flashlight as if I had just discovered fire. They pointed at it and exclaimed in words we did not understand. Next, I pressed the on button on my recorder. They eyed it suspiciously until I played back their voices. Then their eyes widened and they pressed their palms to their open mouths. They must have thought I was the Witch of the West.

That evening we took a walk in the area around the hotel. The streets were grim with only a few tiny dimly-lit shops selling an odd mixture of crayons, pots, sponges, candy, and Mao hats. The only food we noticed for sale were mountains of cabbages piled on nearly every street corner—the guide told me later that this was the main staple for the winter season. What left the greatest impression on me were old lotus-footed women whose feet had obviously been bound. They tiptoed and swayed side to side, making tiny steps, supported on each arm by younger women. That was the moment when imperial China's legacy came to life for me. I was truly in another time and place.

♦♦♦

The Beijing zoo was never meant to be a highlight, but my group really wanted to see it and all the other zoos along our route. Each member seemed to be in the habit of collecting zoos like others collect baseball cards, antiques, or even spouses.

Even on a short bus ride, the good doctor needed her nicotine fix, and she lit up to the protests of the group. A chorus of "we were told there would be no smoking on the bus" filled the small space like an explosive. I asked her to put out the cigarette, but she took her time, mumbling under her breath. I knew that I'd have to confront Ms. Doctor privately. I was not about to chastise her in public, though her inconsiderate actions were already affecting the cohesion of my group. As it was, I worried about how I'd keep peace among them. When I'd noticed in our first dinner conversation that the group consisted of a flammable mix of staunch liberals and ultra conservatives, I'd vowed to keep all conversations strictly on the topic of animals. The minute I'd hear someone raise a political flag, I'd find a way to jump in with panda information. "Did you know that a panda needs to consume more than forty pounds of bamboo each day because bamboo is so nutritionally poor? That pandas mark their territory with a scent gland located beneath the tail?" It was like giving them candy.

The Beijing zoo, similar in size to the Bronx Zoo, was filled with outmoded cages that no American zoo visitor would have found tolerable, but with over a billion people to feed it was understandable: zoo exhibitions were not a priority. We found only one unforgettable exhibit: a cage filled with a motley assortment of domestic dogs and puppies, yapping and jumping at the wire mesh separating them from the visitors, for whom this seemed a favorite place to gawk. No other exhibit attracted such crowds.

Our second night at the hotel brought yet another adventure, courtesy of the doctor. Evidently, she had brought a bottle of her favorite alcoholic beverage in that large bag and had more than a nip before she lit her final cigarette for the night. She fell into a drunken slumber with the cigarette burning in her hand, and the bedding caught fire. Although the hotel didn't have anything as revolutionary as smoke alarms, the hall minder on night duty—they had one stationed on each floor—smelled the smoke. Ms. Doctor was shaken awake unscathed, though the smoke-filled room was a shambles, with charred furniture and smoldering curtains.

In the morning, I was informed by the hotel manager that my group would not be released from the hotel until I, personally, paid an astronomical sum of money for the damages. I saw my plans for a new car going up in smoke, and the group was up in arms. "We won't miss our flight to Xian, will we?" For once, they were united. What to do? I did not have that kind of cash, so I called the travel agent in the US to seek advice. "You have got to send her back," he said over the sputtering connection.

"Back?" I asked. "To the U.S.?" I was incredulous. "But she paid a fortune for this trip. Will she get a refund?" I didn't really want to defend her, but I couldn't envision myself taking such a drastic step. She seemed so angry, she might bop me on the head with her bottle.

"No, no refund," he said. "It's all in the rules she agreed to. They all did," he said categorically. "And I'll take care of the damages, for now. She'll pay later. Give me the hotel manager."

I was only slightly relieved. I still had to confront her and dreaded her reaction. Would she scream? Did she have a bionic arm she hadn't told me about? To my surprise, she was like a contrite child sitting there in the hotel lobby twirling an unlit cigarette. She hung her head down, pressed her lips together, and did not argue. She knew she'd violated more than one rule and acquiesced to being put on the next plane without so much as a "but." Good riddance, I thought, thinking it would be another anecdote for my journal.

I'd been writing in the journal each evening, recording this trip, because I didn't want to forget even the tiniest detail. Everything here was so different, we might as well have been on Saturn, or even another solar system. That evening I sat down to record my impressions of the day, but the little red bound notebook was not on my nightstand where I left it each night.

"Um, Dad? Did you move my journal?" I asked.

"No, what gave you that idea? Maybe it fell down. Did you look under the bed?"

I spent the next two hours tearing apart all our suitcases. It was nowhere.

"I have an idea of what happened," my father said, snapping his fingers. "They must have taken it to have it checked!"

"What? Checked for what?"

"Don't forget, we are in communist country. There's no freedom of expression here," he said, and I knew he was speaking from experience.

Oh, my God, what did I write? I tried to recall if there was anything that could land me in prison. Did I badmouth the canine zoo exhibit? Say anything improper about the airport guards? Criticized the dimness of the hotel?

"Look, I have experience with these kinds of bullies," my father said. "Speak to the floor minder and ask her if she has it. Be polite but firm."

"If she does, she won't admit it, Dad."

"Yes, but you have to let them know you are wise to their tricks," he waved his arm as if I needed to be persuaded.

In the morning, I saw the manager again and told him my journal was missing and that I wanted it back. He looked at me with narrowed eyes. "Who would want your journal? I'll ask the chambermaid," he said. After breakfast, he found me and said, "No one has seen it. You must have lost it."

"I did not lose it. You have it," I blurted out, my blood boiling. I decided to reverse his threat. "I will not move my group out of this hotel until you find it."

In the evening, my journal magically appeared on my night table. I shuffled through the pages, but nothing seemed to be missing. I resolved to be more careful in the way I characterized my impressions. Maybe I'd write in code, or in Yiddish!

♦ ♦ ♦

After seeing many wonders in Beijing, such as the Temple of Heaven and the Forbidden City, we moved on to several more cities, stopping to see a wide range of uninspiring, poorly-designed zoos with sad-looking animals. But we enjoyed visiting renowned cultural sites: the Great Wall at Badaling, the terracotta soldiers of Xi'an, the mystical mountains of Guilin, and the night cruise on the Pearl River in Canton, finally arriving in Chengdu, the provincial capital of Sichuan province, home to the darlings of the conservation community—pandas. With the doctor gone, the group was more cohesive and we were all very excited about our upcoming panda adventure in the Wolong reserve. At dinner, we toasted the pandas with multiple courses of some mysterious Chinese liquor.

◆ ◆ ◆

"Only six!" our Chinese minder informed me on the morning of our Wolong panda reserve day. "Only six permitted to enter the restricted area!" There was a hard edge to his voice and I hoped that no one in my group had heard him.

"But sir!" I pleaded and argued, which only made his eyes darken.

He stood stiffer. "Only six can come in. Take it or leave it." He straightened the sleeves of his drab olive uniform.

Seriously? I wanted to ask. That's less than half of us! But my job was on the line. I decided to turn to my dad for advice.

I left the bureaucrat, fuming, and called my dad to my cavernous hotel room, down an endless hallway, monitored at all times by a squat woman.

"I'm so frustrated," I said, near tears, and told him about the surprise announcement, "These officials make me crazy. What would you do?"

"*Achh*, don't worry. It's not the worst thing in the world not to see pandas. There is so much more to China than just the animals."

"Yeah, like what?"

"*Oy*, don't be silly." He patted my hand and smiled. "I was speaking to some of the group members the other morning and heard they would love to visit the Stone Forest in Yunnan Province," he said.

"Stone Forest? But it's not on our itinerary."

"Exactly! You should tell the Chinese official that they will need to rearrange it since they disappointed your group."

"But, but... what about the pandas?"

"If you are asking me, no one should go. It's only fair. They won't mind as much if none of them goes. At worst, they'll be angry with the Chinese, not with you."

I was glad to have a solution, but worried that the bureaucrats may not take kindly to being forced to alter the itinerary so drastically. The Stone Forest was in Yunnan, more than 500 miles away!

But Dad's ploy worked.

We flew to Kunming, where a sumptuous feast was set for our group on the second floor of the best local restaurant. As in some of the other restaurants we had visited, the most elegant dining room with mirrored walls, starched table linens, and porcelain dishes was on the second floor. The first floor, decent but far from elaborate, was reserved for party members, while the ground floor was the plainest, with beat-up wooden tables and rickety chairs, specifically for workers.

Our meal consisted of many platters of beautiful dishes whose ingredients, while tasty, were not identifiable. I knew better than to ask what we were eating. For the grand finale, two servers in bright blue uniforms trimmed in gold braid carried a platter so huge that each end was supported on their shoulders. They set it on the table with great pride and ceremony, but when my group saw dozens of fried grasshoppers with their legs up in the air in what appeared to be chocolate sauce, they shrank in horror.

"Please, you must make them take it away!" several of them said. "I will gag if it's not off the table this minute," another agreed. I was embarrassed at such cultural insensitivity, but honestly, I knew no one, including me, would sample the delicacy. I knew other cultures ate insects and couldn't understand why we Americans were so grossed out by them—except for Rob. I mumbled something about allergies and watched as they removed the platter, casting strange glances at us.

Next afternoon our group was amazed to see the magnificent works of nature that made up the Stone Forest—odd, geologic limestone karsts formed 270 million years ago. The extraordinary pillars and stalagmites carved by weather were incredible. True, they were not fluffy pandas, but they stretched as far as the eye could see and, like the pandas, were part of nature's bounty. The stone sculptures and the colorful costumes of the local tribal Yi people provided plenty of distraction for my group.

Our last stop on this trip was the luxurious Shangri-La Hotel in Hong Kong. Its comforts —an individual butler assigned to each room—made my chicks forget any inconveniences of the trip, and the happy hour I treated them to each night did not hurt either. In the end, the pandas remained ghosts of our imagination, and everyone's desire to see them in the flesh only grew. The public clamor for rented pandas grew in the decade after our trip—perhaps even fueled by the trustees who were in my group— until several zoos, including the San Diego Zoo, Zoo Atlanta, and Smithsonian's National Zoo acquired them. Except for the six-month loan in 1987, the Bronx Zoo stuck to a no-panda policy and focused, instead, on helping our Chinese colleagues develop panda conservation strategies.

Chapter 15

Speaking in Tongues

I had heard about the mysterious mynah bird and looked forward to getting one, whether it spoke or not. Our department's collection of handleable birds was small, and adding another species would give us more opportunity to vary our animal demonstrations. As for its ability to speak, I knew only that mynahs had a voice curiously similar in sound to humans and that they were accurate mimics whose vocabulary could reach as many as one hundred words. It was not known at the time if they had any cognition linked to these words, or whether the words were associated with certain events or behaviors in the owners' homes. By now behavioral scientists believe that such an association exists.

This mynah's owner had died, and although the zoo didn't usually accept such donations—taking in strays would divert funds, time, and attention from critical priorities, plus unwanted pets are often in poor health and may bring diseases to zoo populations—this time, we had. Most such callers are

redirected to animal shelters and other organizations dedicated to this purpose. However, this caller, a relative of the deceased, was quite concerned that the animal would die of a broken heart if it wasn't taken in and cared for with the sensitivity he believed it deserved. He felt that given this bird's unparalleled vocabulary, it should not be thrust into an uncertain fate.

I don't know what exactly softened the zoo clerk who took the original call, but eventually the matter was routed to the director. Given his well-known interest in birds, he couldn't resist such a tempting offer. The whole affair was kept rather hush-hush, to discourage any other animal owners from making offers to the zoo.

After the appropriate quarantine period to ensure that it harbored no diseases, the mynah finally made its appearance in the director's office. To his disappointment, initially at least, the animal was mute. Except for the usual kinds of noises that a bird might make, the new arrival was quiet. Who knows? Maybe it was traumatized by the loss of its owner. The bird curators counseled patience. "Give it time, it may yet show its talents," they advised.

In the meantime, the mynah seemed to be getting more comfortable in its new digs and its food was almost certainly superior. Fresh fruit, seeds, and crickets appeared regularly, sometimes accompanied by its favorite snack of all—figs. But it still had nothing to say. Its black feathers, which looked dull on arrival, now shone and its reddish-yellow beak and yellow eye patches contrasted artistically with the plumage. What a perfect specimen it would be, if only…

Finally, the day came. The mynah began repeating a phrase that sounded clearly intentional, rather than accidental. The phrase seemed to consist of four words, but for the life of him, the director could not make them out. He listened carefully each time the bird vocalized, but the words—if one could call them that—were elusive. Perhaps the sounds are not words after all, he speculated. Maybe they are just gibberish. In frustration, he called in the bird curators. They too listened carefully, but couldn't make sense of the mynah's utterances. "Could it be some sort of a foreign language?" one of them ventured a guess. But it didn't sound like a language any of them had ever heard.

Wouldn't we all like to be Dr. Doolittle, if just for a moment? We could find out exactly what the animals were thinking, and what their yips, chirps, barks, howls, and songs were all about. It isn't that scientists aren't working to make new discoveries every day. Just recently, scientists analyzed dolphin clicks and chirps and found them to be very similar to and as complex as human vocal communication. Playful growls of dogs have been found to be very different from warning growls to intruders. Argentine horned frog tadpoles scream under water to scare off predators, and elephants' voices contain more nervous shaking when they approach dominant animals, the way a human's voice might convey nervousness when speaking to a boss. Scientists have recorded and compared the rumbles of calm and nervous pachyderms, that's how they know. And just like humans, animals' voices get louder when other noises compete with their conversations. Whales sing louder in waters disturbed by motorboats, and baby birds chirp louder in noisy city environments. Even the lowly chicken can make over twenty different sounds to communicate.

After a while the director became tired of the whole business with the mynah. He had far more important things on his mind: securing funding for new exhibits and placating curators competing for funds. And so, my division acquired the bird.

A bird keeper in his tan uniform came to my office one morning and put the mynah in its cage on my desk. "Here it is, you can keep this dud," he said with a smile and walked out, not waiting for my reply. I was instantly offended on behalf of the mynah. Why he's just being a bird, I thought, doing bird things. He doesn't have to talk. "What's the matter with these people?" I muttered under my breath.

At that very moment the bird decided to reply. Whether it had been the change of venue, or my pressure-free attitude, I couldn't know, but heard distinctly the four mystery words:

"*Gey kakn ofn yam.*"

"What?" I called out, glad no one was yet in the office. I wondered if I had imagined it. A minute passed and to my shock, the mynah repeated the phrase. Now I knew two things for sure. First, its owner had spoken to it in Yiddish, and second, he was not a refined man. Not to speak ill of the dead, but he taught his bird a most indelicate phrase: "Go shit in the ocean," or basically, "Drop dead," or "Go to hell." I pictured him then in his Bronx apartment, an uncouth man, perhaps cursing his wife, or maybe he had someone else in mind he felt compelled to chastise in the most colorful of languages.

I was the only Yiddish-speaker in my office, actually in the entire zoo. I vowed never to reveal the meaning of the mystery phrase. From now on, the bird would be just what he was meant to be: a proud representative of his Asian species. In the months that followed, whenever I'd hear the bird call out in his all-too-human voice, I'd smile mysteriously and be tempted to give him a scolding... in Yiddish, of course.

♦♦♦

Not all animals speak in voices; some are more expressive using body language. At first I couldn't say exactly why I was attracted to a hulking, odd animal with a funny name: *gnu goat* (with a silent g), except that maybe its name reminded me of an Yiddish expression, "*nu*," as in, "Okay already, let's get the show on the road." In zoological circles, the gnu goat is known as a *takin*, but I preferred to call it a gnu goat, fully realizing that it was not the same kind of gnu as the African wildebeest. Its appearance resembled an animal designed by a committee: a nose like a moose, a stance like a bison, and a little beard like a goat. Even its evolutionary lineage is strange. Sometimes described as a goat antelope, it is a creature most closely related to a modern sheep.

But I actually had a lot in common with Gracie the gnu goat, a resident of the Bronx Zoo in the late seventies and early eighties. She came from the same remote part of the world as I did. We had both looked upon the crisp blue sky above the Himalayas in our early years as children of Central Asia, and we both ended up in the Bronx Zoo, thousands of miles away from our birthplace. We also both had a craving for salt, Gracie with her salt lick, me with the ever-present saltshaker on my kitchen table. Gracie the goat antelope was neither a goat nor an antelope. And I was neither an Asian, where I was born and spent my earliest years, nor a blue-blooded American. And so, our one-sided friendship began.

Never one to miss a good opportunity to learn, I took walks on my lunch hour or en route to meetings on the grounds of the verdant 265-acre expanse of the park. In a city filled with brick, cement, steel and glass, observing the beauty of animals was a rare treat for most and a daily opportunity for me. This was why I had accepted the job. As a city dweller, I craved nearness to nature, and though watching animals in zoo enclosures is no substitute for venturing out into the wild, regularly seeing living, breathing creatures was a real privilege. Sometimes it felt better than a cash bonus.

The takin exhibit was quite some distance from my office. On the way there, I'd pass the Reptile House where most middle schoolers ran to first. Next, I'd skirt around the World of Darkness, where mammal department curators using their intimate knowledge of nocturnal animal needs and habits had figured out how to simulate night. Here, fruit-eating bats known as flying foxes dined on a fortified fruit diet; porcupines foraged on the forest floor for roots; and galagos (also known as bush babies) scrounged for insects—all thinking it was dinnertime, even though for visitors it was daytime.

Well before I approached the takin enclosure, I could smell her pungent musky smell, which many would describe as foul. Looking at her shaggy golden-grayish coat and the short blondish fringe under her chin, I wondered if she longed to be with her family grazing on a rugged Asian mountain slope. Takins are unusual in that, unlike most other forest ungulates (hoofed mammals), they are gregarious.

It was summer, and in her native land she would have migrated with her group to an alpine meadow to feed on grasses and leaves. She approached the fence with her head low, swaying as she strolled forward, and stood there assessing me. I noticed her powerful body and horns, something that visitors were often surprised to find in a female. It wouldn't have surprised me if she weighed 500 pounds or more, and she was nearly as tall as my 5'4" frame.

We stood there staring at one another, and then she urinated. I knew she was marking her territory, a behavior often reserved for the males of a species. Territorial behavior in animals doesn't surprise us, but we rarely speak of it in human terms. I noticed that the heads of different zoo departments were equally territorial, defending their turf, and that included me as well. Animals hang on to their territory to protect resources like food or mates; with us it was usually budgets. And like Gracie, I was a territorial female. It always amused me how observing animals often made me reflect on humans.

Gracie made a low whistling sound through her flared black nostrils and I took it as a sign that she was displeased with my visit. I went on my way, but there was something so dignified in her stance that I made a point of coming by to see her again whenever the opportunity arose to take this remote path.

I did so several times, each time noticing more of Gracie's features: her black muzzle, her deliberate gait, and her cautious eyes. Her lustrous coat especially intrigued me for its role in the legend of the Golden Fleece. I'm a sucker for literary references, particularly those that pertain to animals. If Jason and the Argonauts had set out on the arduous journey to acquire the fleece, then it must have been considered priceless even a thousand years ago by the spinners of myths. Gracie and I weren't exactly becoming friends, but I felt she was not as threatened by my presence.

Later that year an errand took me to the same part of the park, but I was in a hurry so I took my trusty chariot—an electric golf cart. As the cart neared the exhibit, Gracie charged forcefully at the fence, which shook at the impact, and a cloud of dust rose in the air behind her. I couldn't tell if she was excited to see me or wanted to drive me back. I backed up a bit, crunching on the fall leaves, then moved forward again, and once more Gracie charged towards the cart as if I were a potential predator. Was she thinking I resembled an Asiatic black bear, a leopard, or a tiger—her natural enemies?

I backed up the cart and took another path, not wanting to alarm Gracie any more, but her fierce exhibition made me think of the unnatural intrusions on her native habitat. They wouldn't be driving electric carts, but hordes of tourists and bush meat hunters threaten Gracie's wild habitat in China, Bhutan, northeast India, and northern Myanmar. The habitat and the animals it supports are shrinking rapidly because of deforestation.

Several months later, I walked past the exhibit and noticed that Gracie was gone. What happened? Was she sick? I inquired when I got back to the office, but received only a partially satisfying answer: Gracie had been shipped away from the zoo. No one told me exactly where she went, but I knew that zoos exchanged individuals on breeding loans, and hoped she went to a facility where she would meet a male and produce a healthy calf with a white blaze on its forehead and a dark stripe running down its back.

CHAPTER 16

Tess of Berkovits's

It was true. An Airedale terrier was featured in the special "Pet of the Week" column. I had to admit that it was quite rare to have such a good-looking, apparently healthy purebred animal dumped in a shelter. What was the story behind it? I wondered.

Ten-year-old Jeremy was jumping up and down, unable to conceal his excitement.

"I don't know," I said, "I'll discuss it with Dad."

"Oh, Mom, please!" Jeremy pleaded and looked for aid to his older sister.

A few months earlier, when her brother had started rallying for a dog and their father's allergies had come up, she'd been the one to first mention this breed. A future lawyer, she had an answer for everything. "There are dogs that don't shed. My friend told me about Airedales and poodles."

"Ugh, I don't want a poodle. They look so stupid with those pom-pom tails." Jeremy had had his own idea of a boy's dog.

But now, as a very sweet-looking canine face stared back from *The Journal News*, and Jeremy was sold.

"I have an idea," Jessica said. "Let's not get it right away. Let's just pay a visit to the shelter. Maybe we won't even like him."

◆◆◆

In the several months that had passed, filled with regular "I want a dog" whining sessions, I hadn't broken down yet. My job was all-consuming and David's commute to work in lower Manhattan added three hours to his workdays. We were too tired to assume the care of another living being. By now my children had heard enough of my lectures and actually had some experience caring for small pets. It wouldn't have surprised me if they could recite chapter and verse every admonishment I had ever mentioned.

But that Saturday, after seeing the "Pet of the Week" column, I swallowed the bait. The terminal cuteness of the animal in the photo began to melt my resolve, but I still hoped that someone else had already adopted it, or that he would turn out to have a mean disposition that would save me. I did not show any softening in my position to the kids as we piled into our station wagon and headed to the Sound Shore Animal Shelter.

Upon our arrival, the caretaker asked us to fill out several questionnaires aimed at ascertaining our suitability as adopters. I was pleased with the care they took. When my husband mentioned that I worked at the Bronx Zoo, the caretaker seemed ready to skip the formalities, but I completed the paperwork. She then eagerly introduced us to Tess, a two-year old Airedale with sad eyes and a stump of a tail.

"You know, these dogs don't even shed," she said casually, as if she and the kids had conspired.

"Really?" David was glad to hear this and patted the dog's back. She looked up at him soulfully and licked his hand. He patted her again and the little stump of a tail waved furiously.

"She likes us!" Jeremy exclaimed. David and I looked at one another, trying to communicate with our eyes.

"We rarely get purebreds like this one," the shelter woman remarked, trying to help us with the decision. "Her owner couldn't control her. She kept getting out, running off, and making him pay for too many leash law tickets."

"That was his fault, not the dog's," Jessica said, bolstering her case. "Isn't it up to the owner to put the leash on?"

"We would be much more fair with this dog," Jeremy continued the lobbying campaign.

"OK, OK," David said, looking at me. "What's her name again?"

"Tess, like *Tess of the d' Urbervilles*, if you read that novel," the shelter caretaker said.

A dog with a literary provenance, I thought. That *is* unusual. I couldn't think of a single dog named Tess. "Yes, we will take her," I said.

◆ ◆ ◆

On her arrival to our home, Tess ran into the yard with glee and promptly caught a squirrel. We didn't see her bloody deed until we found her standing over the carcass, licking her chops, with bits of blood on her blond beard and her remnant of a tail wagging. Though at forty-five pounds she was small for her breed and had sustained a limp due to some mishap with her former owner, perhaps even due to abuse, she was feisty and her life list included dozens of raccoons chased into sewers on our evening walks.

Tess was full of surprises. She had a penchant for licking our velvet sofas until they were soaked with saliva, but she did this only when were out of the house. She was a perfect lady when we were home and never attempted to jump onto the furniture, but we often spotted her through our porch window jumping off the sofa as we were about to enter.

Tess had a vulnerable side too. I noticed that she disappeared during a thunderstorm when she was still new to our home. "Did you let her out, David?" I asked, after I looked all through the house and she was nowhere to be seen.

"You must be kidding," he said. "Who in their right mind would let a dog out in this weather?"

"OK, so help me look for her."

We scoured the basement first because it had many hiding places. Nothing. Then we returned upstairs because of a faint noise in our bedroom. By then the thunder shower had let up, and we saw something moving under the bed-skirt of our bed. Her terrified eyes peered out at us. Apparently, she had run to hide under the bed in the storm, but could not get out when it abated. We hauled her out and gave her some biscuits. The stump of her tail wagged gratefully. She would continue this behavior during every storm.

My father, who stayed with us on the weekends, was very fond of Tess, even after a skunk sprayed him from head-to-toe as he tried to get Tess away from it on one of their evening walks. She had chased the skunk up a tree and was not giving up. Several cans of tomato juice rescue clean-up later, he laughed and said, "Tess is gutsy and no one's fool."

Despite my initial resistance, my affection for her grew, in no small part because of her fetching antics and charm. Though she was loved by everyone in our household, Tess was Jeremy's best friend. And true to Jeremy's promise, he took excellent care of Tess for a decade.

◆◆◆

When he graduated from high school, Jeremy attended an international program in peace studies that included a visit with Pope John Paul at the Vatican. While he was away for a year, Tess, who had been getting more and more arthritic over the years, took a serious turn for the worse. We dreaded the thought of having to explain to Jeremy on his return that his old friend was gone. After we had exhausted all of the remedies we could think of, I decided to do something that violated zoo rules. Employee's individual pets were not allowed to enter the zoo grounds for health reasons and could not be cared for by the zoo's veterinarian.

I knew that if anyone could help our suffering Tessie, it was Dr. Emil Dolensek, a professional with a vast knowledge of his field, but also a man who truly loved every single living creature. He was not merely a highly-qualified medical technician, he was also unusually compassionate and gentle. The way he communicated with sick animals, who could not describe their symptoms, one would have to conclude he was actually Dr. Doolittle in disguise.

Tess was always eager for a car ride, but that last time she was too sick to climb in, so we lifted her up onto the back seat. She had lost a considerable amount of weight and was a shadow of the forty-five pounds of muscle and brawn we had picked up at the shelter. I drove to the zoo heartbroken and took her in through the back gate directly to the veterinary compound. Emil met me and lifted Tess out. He spoke to her softly and took her into his suite.

He injected her with saline because she was dehydrated and spent an inordinate amount of time massaging the areas where the fluid accumulated in pockets under her skin. She stood silently looking at him as he spoke to her non-stop. In adjacent rooms, sick crocodiles needed tending, a stork was in for the repair of a broken bill and a hippo was recuperating from foot surgery. But for Emil at that moment, Tess was the most important animal. After he had examined Tess, he told me that she was suffering. "Leave her with me overnight. I'll do whatever I can to ease her pain, but if not… " I didn't let him finish. I knew that if Emil could not save her, no one would.

Tess never left the zoo. It was a long time before I could bring myself to tell Jeremy the sad news. I remembered Hermie the Crab and didn't have the heart to announce her death on the phone, so I waited until I could do it in person, months later. Jeremy was devastated. Several years later he found another rescued dog, a mutt named Waverly. And though he loved her, she could never quite replace Tess, his first canine friend. The "pet of the week" had become the "pet of a lifetime."

CHAPTER 17

The Archbishop and the Gibnut

Our plane sat on the tarmac and I anxiously craned my neck to follow the luggage wagon moving below. From the stylized macaw logo on its side I could tell it was carrying our important cargo—cartons of books and other teaching materials we were bringing to Belize. My staff and I were surprised and honored when the government of Belize, focused on preserving its remarkable fauna and the world's second longest barrier reef, requested our assistance in revitalizing the national curriculum in support of conservation goals. And what magnificent creatures they had to protect: jaguars, ocelots, macaws, sharks, and corals, just to name a few. Here was an opportunity to take our programs, which had shown such success in U.S. schools, and adapt them to a new culture and the realities of teaching in a developing country. We were excited, but had a lot of questions: Would this kind of experiment work? Were our classroom activities culturally relevant? I wasn't sure, but was determined to try.

I assembled a group of our finest teacher trainers to conduct the first-ever environmental education training workshops for school principals and science education leaders representing each of Belize's districts. In turn, they would train their teachers, who'd pass on the novel learning strategies to their students. What gave me hope that the program might succeed were the curricula we had spent years designing: *Pablo Python Looks at Animals*, *Diversity of Lifestyles*, and *Survival Strategies*. Each targeted a different age group and each incorporated games and classroom simulations the kids could not resist. The youngest students followed a friendly mascot, a wise, highly observant snake named Pablo, on their animal adventures. He showed them how to discover the animals' secrets. The more advanced students had to manage wildlife reserves by designing zoos and making decisions about which species to breed. If they could not accommodate the offspring within their space and budget, they had to manage a trade with another zoo. In some instances, they modeled the work of the International Whaling Commission and had to set limits on hunting, then deal with the objections from various communities. It was a new way of teaching: putting kids in the central role of making decisions, planning courses of action, and taking responsibility for outcomes. There was only one rub: the teachers would not be accustomed to giving up so much control. That's why they needed to become comfortable with our techniques.

As I watched the baggage handlers lift the suitcases and bulging bags and pile them into the hold of the plane, something tumbled off the back of the cart. I looked more closely: those were the boxes of our curricula! The cart pulled forward and sped off, leaving our boxes on the tarmac. I tried to get the flight attendant's attention, but she was busy demonstrating how to fasten a seatbelt. Now I knew why my friends had teased me when I told them we'd be flying on the South American carrier TACA. "Take A Chance Airlines," they'd said and laughed. When we'd boarded, each female passenger was presented with a single red rose. What an enchanting start, I'd thought then; now I was frantic. When the flight attendant finally came over, our plane was pulling away, leaving the boxes sitting lonely on the pavement.

"Oh, don't worry," she told me. "They'll catch up."

♦ ♦ ♦

When we stepped off the plane in Belize City, we followed the crowd into the smallest passport control area I had seen. It was a sauna; the air was saturated with moisture. The lines were a jumble, with no order at all, but people laughed and chatted and no one seemed to be in a hurry. All I wanted to know was whether our cartons of teaching materials would ever arrive. I was more concerned about them than my suitcase, though I desperately wanted to shed my jacket and change into something lighter.

En route to the hotel, my colleagues and I discussed alternate approaches to the training in case our materials were delayed—or worse yet, lost! "C'mon guys, we're a creative bunch, we've got to come up with something," I urged. Our friendly cab driver with cocoa skin laughed and said something, but we couldn't understand him. We found out later he spoke Belizean Creole, a mixture of English and West African languages common in this country.

Our Belizean coordinator met us at the hotel to help settle us in and assured us breezily that our materials would arrive—sooner, or later. She said, "When the workshops are launched tomorrow, there will be a surprise."

"What kind of a surprise?" I asked, unsure that I liked the idea.

"Now, how would it be a surprise if I told you?" A radiant smile lit her face. "But I will give you a hint: there will be television cameras."

Cameras! I tensed. I knew we were government guests, but hadn't expected such a high-profile welcome. I had been in front of television cameras before, but not in a foreign country, trying something I wasn't sure would succeed.

None of us could make sense of it, so we had no choice but to try to relax. A thicket of fuchsia-colored bougainvillea around the Mopan hotel emitted a sweet, honeysuckle-like fragrance, and the rum punch served to us on arrival by a charming, ruddy-faced host began to take effect. In a thick Scottish brogue, he assured us that everything here was done on Belize time and that it would help us if we managed to shed our New York haste.

Refilling our glasses, he regaled us with tales of various biologists and marine scientists who lodged there regularly on their way into the wild to carry out field work. Their personal imbroglios—secret girlfriends, famous lovers— turned out to be as fascinating as their research. He showed us a bar chair with our institution's initials—NYZS—carved into it. "See, they all come through here. I get 'em ready for the wild," he bragged.

It would be later, when we had spent some tranquil evenings under the stars with the scientists and more rum, that we fully appreciated just how much stamina it takes to track an animal like the jaguar, a stealthy predator that prefers to do its killing after dark. We also learned first-hand how human activity has imperiled the world's second longest barrier reef—a real underwater rainforest. Scuba divers there regaled us with their tales of eerie, blue-tinged waters with walls and channels of corals in every color of the rainbow pulsating with life: 500 species of fish, manatees, turtles, crustaceans, sponges, and crocodiles. Even the brown boobies, pelicans, and magnificent frigate birds had starring roles in the "happy hour" accounts of these Caribbean raconteurs.

♦♦♦

A rooster's crowing woke me at five the next morning. I was glad not to have to worry if my alarm would go off. Accompanied by our charming Belizean host, we arrived at the workshop location early, not expecting any participants to be there. To my surprise a good number of them were there by seven, bright and eager for the big day ahead. A television station crew arrived soon after, running cables and positioning cameras. Holy cow, the entire workshop would be televised and broadcast on Belize TV. And our materials—were they stranded in New York, hovering somewhere over the Caribbean Sea, or waylaid in some Central American airport?

Within moments a heavyset man arrived, sweat already glistening on his forehead. He approached the site coordinator, saying, "I need some help unloading the boxes." Boxes? I thought hopefully.

Sure enough, I peered outside and saw a jeep stacked with our cartons. I knew them by our WIZE logo, and was so happy that our Wildlife Inquiry through Zoo Education packages had made it on time, all the way to the tropics via the JFK tarmac.

As the crowd of men and women swelled in the room, I continued to welcome each newcomer and introduce myself and my staff. The men were dressed plainly in khakis and T-shirts, the women in colorful cotton skirts. They all seemed happy to be there, and many repeated a variation of, "I can't believe I was selected for this, it's such an honor." They came from all parts of the country, some from as far as Orange Walk Town in the northeast, some from Dangriga, and others from as far away as Punta Gorda in the south. Some had traveled by bus, others had hitchhiked to the dormitory where they'd stay with us for the week-long workshop.

A loud commotion outside alerted me that something big was happening. The crowd parted and an elaborately dressed clergyman walked in. The man's purple cassock and gold cross dangling from a thick chain set off his brown complexion. He looked handsome and self-assured.

"This is Annette and her staff," the coordinator introduced me.

"Annette, meet Archbishop McMillan." I gulped, having never met a cleric of such high rank. I was quite ignorant of the proper etiquette and unsure how to address him. Should I bow? Curtsey? Call him "Your Excellency?" or "Your Grace?"

We shook hands and he disarmed me completely when he mentioned that his brother-in-law was a colleague at the Bronx Zoo. "Small world," he said with a wide grin, "We are all related."

The coordinator announced that the archbishop had come to bless our workshops and wish us an auspicious beginning. After some prayers, the archbishop made a brief speech about the need to educate Belizeans about the fragility of their wild heritage. The audience erupted into enthusiastic applause.

Before he left us, the archbishop called me aside and invited me to join him and his wife for dinner at their home that evening. A wife? I had no idea archbishops could marry. I was overwhelmed. I'd be dining with an archbishop! How did one need to behave to observe the right protocol? I wondered. Was there a rule about which fork or spoon to use for certain dishes?

♦ ♦ ♦

By evening, buoyed by the enthusiastic participation of the workshop attendees, my friend Ann and I went to dinner at the bishop's. He had said I could bring a guest, and I needed her moral support. She had a terrific sense of humor and I knew she'd be able to rescue me from any sticky situation. A taxi with a Creole-speaking driver knew exactly where to go. He chatted non-stop but we hardly made out a word. We stopped in front of a modest white-washed house surrounded by palms and bushes of fragrant yellow flowers with shiny dark green leaves.

The archbishop's wife was a small gray-haired woman with a deferential manner. She wore a prim navy dress with a white embroidered collar. All she needed were white gloves and a pillbox hat to complete the British look I knew the Belizeans loved, with Queen Elizabeth as their head of state. We made small talk about the local cuisine and I surprised her when I told her my husband did most of the cooking.

We sat at the lace-covered dinner table, and as the archbishop said grace I looked down into my gold-rimmed dish. Steam rose from the bowl of mustard-yellow soup, which had chunks of green and orange floating on top. It was cow foot soup, with coconut, pumpkin, okra, Jamaican butter beans, and plenty of habanero. I was surprised at how delicious it was and our hostess was clearly pleased with our abundant praise. We chatted about the workshop and I mentioned a participant who was the only one to arrive late. He came in limping; beneath his frayed shorts a wide bandage, with blood oozing at its edges, was wrapped around his calf. "What had happened to him?" they asked, alarmed.

I recounted his tale: the man's wife, learning that he'd be away for an entire week, had hacked him with a machete. "I ran here as fast as I could," the man had reported to us when he arrived, huffing and puffing. We asked him why he hadn't gone to the doctor. "And miss this workshop? Never!" he said with a grin. "I'll be okay."

The archbishop shook his head and said, "I'm sorry to say, this kind of domestic violence is all too common here." I didn't know how to reply, but his wife broke the awkward moment. "I'd better serve the main course."

"Ah, you are lucky, she got a nice fat gibnut at the market today. They are not so easy to come by," the archbishop said. I smiled and looked toward Ann, who reciprocated my look that said, "what *is* that?" I imagined it to be one of the nearly 500 species of local fish.

Moments later the archbishop's wife walked in, ceremoniously holding a large platter she set in the center of the table. "Please, help yourselves to the gibnut and rice and beans." It sure did not look like fish. It seemed to be some sort of meat, though I could not discern its original shape. Gingerly, I placed a small portion on my plate. "Please, help yourself to more, we don't eat like birds around here," the archbishop encouraged.

"Thank, you, it looks delicious," I said, though I wasn't anxious to sink my teeth into an unknown meat. This is not China, they don't eat dog here, I calmed myself and cut a piece. It seemed gristly. I put a bite in my mouth, chewing slowly and deliberately, willing myself to swallow. The archbishop looked at me expectantly waiting for the verdict. "Nice flavor," I said, swallowing, trying to focus on the abundant garlic instead of the unfamiliar texture.

"If I may ask, your grace, what is a gibnut?" I ventured and lifted another forkful.

His smile widened revealing a set of healthy white teeth. "Why it's a paca. Here we call them gibnut."

"Hmm... I see," I said, trying not to choke on the morsel in my mouth, willing myself not to embarrass my venerable institution by upchucking this well-seasoned wild rodent! I took a deep breath and hoped that Ann, across the table from me, did not know which mammalian order the paca belonged to!

I took a deep breath and came up with a reasonable excuse to stop eating the chewy rodent. "I spied a gorgeous coconut cake in the kitchen. I want to save room for it, hope you don't mind." I flashed a smile, praying it was believable.

When we left, I told Ann what we had eaten. She nearly barfed onto my lap. "Don't be so disgusted yet," I said, "Let's check at the hotel if I'm right about the paca."

Back at the hotel, I asked our friendly bartender about it. He erupted into howls of laughter, "Everyone knows that's the Royal Rat. It was even served to the queen of England when she visited here. It is a delicacy reserved for esteemed guests." I wasn't sure if I should laugh or be ashamed that I hadn't given the gibnut its proper due. Instead I grimaced and the bartender promptly handed me some rum punch. "Here's a chaser!"

When we returned to the U.S., I researched the consumption of rodents around the world and discovered that 89 species of rodents, from pacas to prairie dogs, guinea pigs, mole rats, cloud rats, sand rats, and even dormice supplement the human diet around the world.

In the end, the gibnut episode was eclipsed by images of the reef's pristine waters, the profusion of bougainvillea, and the friendly faces of Belizeans. Most of all, the single most moving moment of the trip was when our workshop participants departed, some with tears in their eyes, carrying the forty-pound cartons of materials on their heads as they walked the two miles to the nearest bus stop. We had made deep connections here, and in future years would host these educators for advanced training sessions in New York.

CHAPTER 18

What's in a Name?

Take the word *rodent*. If you are like most people, you are likely seeing a gray creature with a long naked tail that roams sewers and subways and spreads diseases like the bubonic plague—in other words, a rat: *Rattus rattus* (black) and *Rattus norvegicus* (brown). Now, if you hear the word *squirrel*, you'll conjure a sweet fuzzy critter sitting in a park on its haunches grasping a peanut in its front paws and looking perfectly adorable with its extravagant bushy tail laid over its back like a mink stole. Both creatures are rodents, yet one evokes repulsion, the other sympathy. I've often wondered why in our pop culture squirrels always play the sympathetic roles—Rocket J. Squirrel, Bullwinkle's friend; Skunny and his girlfriend Rosie—while rats are the villains. Who can forget Templeton in *Charlotte's Web*, Professor Rattigan in *The Great Mouse Detective*, and the rat villains in *The Tale of Despereaux*?

They may be cute, but as it happens, I've had a love-hate relationship with squirrels.

◆◆◆

One of the first things I noticed when I began working at the zoo was the way urban children, especially those from the inner city, became excited when they chanced upon a gray squirrel. And we had lots of these charming rodents roaming the zoo grounds. Of course, they were not on exhibit, but being native to the eastern part of the country, they found plentiful acorns and hickory nuts in our forested 265-acre park.

It was always such a moving sight to see a group of rowdy fifth graders stop dead in their tracks, cease their yelling, and move cautiously toward a squirrel scampering down a tree head first, stopping to pick up an acorn and waving its silver-tipped tail in victory. They watched, totally silent as if they were field scientists encountering a rare wild specie for the first time. Every time I saw this I had two thoughts: one, that it was depressing that these children were so removed from nature that a squirrel could hold their attention as much as a lion. They reminded me of myself as young girl, nature deprived, growing up in an industrial city. And two, that all children possess an uncanny ability to observe with the keenness of a scientist, if they are presented with something interesting.

◆◆◆

It wasn't just children who were fascinated with squirrels. One day my father—an eighty-six-year-old kid—sat on the second-story terrace of our suburban house, which was bordered by tall beech trees, and stared intently at the branches that hung over the railing. "What are you looking at Dad?" I asked, following his gaze to find a squirrel that scurried down to sit on the railing, twitching its whiskers and holding its tail up like an umbrella to shade it from the sun.

"Do you have any unshelled peanuts?" my dad asked.

"No, but I have peanut butter. Do you want some?"

He laughed. "No, no, I need the whole nuts with shells on. Can you get me some?"

"Sure, but what do you need them for?"

"You'll see."

I bought what he wanted and promptly forgot about it. One day when I returned from work, I found him sitting on the terrace looking steadily at his watch, then shifting his gaze toward the terrace railing.

"What are you doing, Dad?"

"Shh… be quiet. You'll disturb my experiment," he whispered with a look of intense concentration.

And then I noticed it. A chubby squirrel with a luxurious tail sat at one end of the railing holding a peanut in its dainty paws, whiskers trembling. At the other end of the railing lay a small stash of nuts.

"I'm timing how long it takes to eat one peanut and then how long before it goes for the next one. I already timed its friend."

And so began his hobby as an amateur naturalist. The sight of him chomping on a peanut once his experiment was done made him look as adorable to me as the critters he was observing.

♦♦♦

One evening, lying in bed after a particularly tiring day at the office and wanting desperately to get enough sleep, I heard a noise somewhere near the ceiling. Maybe I'm imagining these sounds, I thought, only half awake. But they continued, and soon began to sound like running, scurrying little feet. Am I really awake, I wondered? I nudged my husband. "I hate to wake you honey," I said.

"What's wrong?" He asked, rubbing his eyes.

"Listen."

"What? I don't hear anything."

"Listen again," I said,

"Oh, that? I bet we have a squirrel in the attic," he mumbled and turned over on his side, snoring within moments.

Until then I had never contemplated the possibility that rodents could move in with us. It disturbed me greatly. How many were there? I hoped it was just one. I was disgusted and decided that in the morning I'd take care of this intruder.

The next morning, I said to David, "So how do you propose we get rid of it?"

"Who?"

"You know, the beast in the attic," I said, irritated at his lack of urgency.

"The squirrel? How should I know? You are the animal expert," he said picking up his cup of coffee.

"OK, I will ask someone at the zoo," I said, remembering that before his morning coffee, the poor guy was useless.

♦ ♦ ♦

I wasn't too worried. I knew David would figure something out. We had always been proud of our modest brick cape sitting on a quiet street, with its flowering quince and carpet of purple bugleweed spikes in the spring. David had labored for years perfecting our nest, working on it when he had time, evenings and weekends. I called him "The Man with the Golden Hands." In his professional life, he was an engineer and oversaw the Environmental Testing Laboratory of the Port Authority of New York and New Jersey, and later became an expert on port development issues. Yet there was nothing he couldn't do on the home front: diapering a baby, cooking, tiling, plumbing, electrical work, carpentry—he was a true Renaissance man. He replaced two dozen old casement windows with elegant Pellas, built a sky-lit sunroom, installed Italian tile counters that matched the kitchen floor, and demolished a wall that separated our dining area from the kitchen and impeded convenient flow for parties.

I returned from work feeling like the winner of Publisher's House Sweepstakes. One of our animal experts had given me a "Havahart" trap on loan. I had told him that I didn't want to hurt the squirrel, only to send it on a safari elsewhere. He had given me a knowing smile and wished me luck.

"Just be patient, Annette," he counseled.

Patience, shmatience, I thought.

The trap was ingenuous! It was about a foot and a half long, made of sturdy wire mesh with steel reinforcements, and a bonus "gravity action door" and "sensitive trigger" to ensure efficient capture. I was relieved that all its internal edges were smooth to prevent injuries to the critters during transport. I had no idea yet where and how we'd transport our unwelcome visitor, but I felt magnanimous, like a wealthy benefactor with the means to send it on vacation in the country. It felt like we were in on a covert caper. "David, are you ready for action?" I asked that evening.

"Ah... action?" He winked. "Are you asking what I think you are asking?"

"Baiting the trap," I explained and he burst out laughing.

We knew that the squirrel would have to exit at some point to forage, so we placed the trap strategically and baited it with Skippy, my favorite brand of peanut butter.

The next morning, success! A fat squirrel ran back and forth in the trap, searching frantically for an exit.

"Soon enough, my friend," I said to it.

That's when it occurred to me that I had no idea where to release it.

"Where should we take it, David?" I asked.

"Well, let's not let it out too close to our backyard. It's liable to find its way back into the house."

Ooh, I hadn't given that much thought. I had an impulse to run to the library to search for information (it was in the pre-Internet days), but the poor thing was scratching furiously. There was no time.

"You're right, hon, but we're lucky—there are plenty of parks around here."

I was glad that the little fellow in the trap would soon find himself in a lovely new wooded home, with lots of acorns and children to gawk at him.

We got into the car and drove up Boston Post Road. We had the choice of Flint Park, Harbor Island Park, the Marshlands Conservancy, The Rye Nature Center, and several smaller green spaces. We drove slowly for about ten minutes looking for a good spot, but suddenly I felt uneasy. Would someone see me pulling the trap out and releasing the animal? Was it even legal? I had no idea, but we had to get rid of the critter. A notice in the Gannet paper's "From the Police Blotter" section flashed before me: *Bronx Zoo curator arrested for illegal wildlife release.* What shame I'd bring the zoo! I felt nauseous. In the meantime, the squirrel sounded frantic in the back seat, scratching and making chittering sounds.

"Stop here!" I called out to David as we approached the nearest patch of green, not even in the park yet.

Feeling like a thief, or maybe a kidnapper, I hauled the trap out of the back seat, threw open the door, and watched the squirrel prance out joyfully. I hoisted the trap back in and said, "Drive! And fast, let's get the hell out of here."

"What's the hurry?" David asked.

"I have a feeling we've done something illegal."

"For crying out loud, calm down, it's just a squirrel. We haven't released a crocodile. Anyway, it'll blend in with the ones that live here."

My heart thumped in my chest. I did not like skulking around with what may have been contraband.

"I'm glad we're done with it, though," I sighed as we made our way past tree-lined streets and manicured lawns, heading home.

◆◆◆

That night we celebrated with a bottle of Cabernet Sauvignon and a steak dinner. I called my husband "Trapper Dave Extraordinaire," laughingly imagining him in a coonskin hat. It wasn't until well past midnight that the patter of little feet above our bed resumed. I couldn't believe it.

"David, listen! They're back. There are… more," I tapped his back.

"Yes," he said sleepily. "I hear it this time. I'll have to figure out where they are sneaking in and close up the opening."

"When can you do that?"

"Not until the weekend," he sighed.

"Oh no! We're liable to have a dozen by then," I said, but knew that it was impossible for him to take time off work to deal with what were quickly becoming my least favorite animals.

My prediction was prophetic. Over the next several days we trapped a dozen more squirrels—a baker's dozen in all. David found a tiny hole just beneath the roof line and fixed it with a piece of wood, all while teetering on a ladder.

"Thank you, sweetie," I said when he came down. "And congratulations!" I added, as if we'd hit the jackpot.

"I'm just glad we're done," he grumbled. "I'm tired of skulking around getting rid of these rodents. People might start to notice and think we're nuts."

♦ ♦ ♦

It was no wonder the zoo animal expert advised patience, a character trait which is not my forte. The squirrels returned with a vengeance.

"But I closed up the hole, where are they getting in now?" David asked, frustrated.

We were both having the same thought: back to square one.

David hauled out the heavy 20-foot ladder and propped it up, then climbed up and inspected his repair job as I watched, squinting in the sunlight.

He called out, "You won't believe it! The buggers chewed through the thick board I nailed to cover the hole. With amazingly sharp teeth they have!" He put his nose near the opening. "Wheew! It stinks in there. There may be a dozen more. They must've brought their friends."

This is when I knew I had some serious squirrel research to do. Time to hit the library and scour the literature. Sure enough, I discovered that squirrels have an incredibly good sense of smell and that they can find their way back to their nest over great distances, from ten miles or more. So, we had released all of them too close! And not just that, I discovered just how intelligent squirrels are. They've been observed storing their acorns in many different hidden caches they know how to find later, and they've even *pretended* to hide the nuts and then hid them somewhere else when the observer was out of view!

When I came home, I explained the situation to David, who was now quite the experienced trapper. We stood on our front lawn and discussed the situation.

"We've got to catch them and drive them much farther away, in a zigzag line across the highway so the buggers won't outsmart us," I said, resigned to our illicit squirrel-dumping activity. "Maybe this time we should hire one of those stretch limos for the long ride."

"OK, Saxon Woods Park across the New England Thruway, here we come. Or maybe even more northwest to the Silver Lake Preserve across Route 684?" David said, already hatching our new plan.

"And you'll have to close up that hole again," I said, looking up, stating the obvious.

"This time I'll put a piece of aluminum lining under the wood," he said. "Two people with masters' degrees can outsmart a rodent!"

"That's right: survival of the fittest," I agreed.

I glanced up at our oak tree and saw a pair of squirrels chasing one another. They were a lovely sight, but I knew I'd never feel the same about them or their endearing antics, even though their tenacity and exquisite adaptations were pretty impressive.

Watching them chase each other and balance on the branches, I remembered my research had also uncovered an early 1970s *Joy of Cooking* recipe for squirrel: braised with walnut gravy and polenta. It was starting to sound rather good.

CHAPTER 19

Riots and Butterflies

The acrid odor of burning tires stung my eyes. Shouts from groups of youths waving banners emanated from trucks speeding along the road, which was curiously devoid of civilian vehicles—except for ours. Police cars and military jeeps in pursuit added to our anxiety. This was not the way I had envisioned modern, cultured Caracas. What was going on?

I had planned this trip carefully and arrived ready to organize the logistics of the first-ever Pan American Congress on Conservation of Wildlife through Education with our Latin hosts. How could it be that one day after my arrival all hell was breaking loose?

After three decades of relative stability, Venezuela erupted in a violent political spasm on February 27, 1989, when President Carlos Andres Perez put into effect a set of austerity reforms crowned by the elimination of gasoline subsidies, which caused gasoline prices to double overnight. The populace was outraged. Riots began eighteen miles east of Caracas, but by the time we were making our way to our first set of meetings in the city center, they had spread like wildfire throughout the capital.

Along the way, we passed groups of young people burning tires, holding up crudely made posters, and other people screaming and running, while stores were shutting their doors. Chaos.

"What is going on here?" I kept asking our driver, but he was in no mood to discuss.

"Ah, troublemakers, these students," he dismissed them with a wave of his hand and a deep drag on his cigarette. Smoke filled our vehicle, and all I could think about was getting back to the hotel and turning on the television to find out what was going on.

This was to be a big turning point in my career. After a succession of promotions, I was now a full curator. By this point I had developed a knack for raising funds. Hundreds of thousands, then millions rolled in as external evaluations demonstrated the merits of our programs. Our international programs grew as a result, mirroring our local and national success. That year I had secured funding and marshaled support from two dozen partner organizations to bring international educators and scientists to the Pan American Congress, to be held in ten months. And after attending the congress I looked forward to enjoying the wonders of one the most biologically diverse South American countries. With wilderness stretching from the Andes mountains to the Amazon Basin, Venezuela boasted jungles teeming with howler monkeys, giant anteaters, hummingbirds, parrots, macaws, and a splendid palette of hundreds of avian species.

If time permitted, I even planned a trip down the Amazon River basin, replete with manatees, river dolphins, and Orinoco crocodiles. I hoped to spy the troupial, the black-headed, orange-bodied member of the oriole family, Venezuela's national bird.

The only positive in this bizarre situation was that, luckily, I had persuaded David to join me, mostly so he wouldn't have to worry about me. It was well past noon when we made our way to meet with one of our senior scientists stationed in Caracas. I gasped when the driver left us off at the gate, because the place looked like an armored camp. Tall fences hugged the electrical gate, and vicious-sounding dogs barked as if they'd tear intruders into pieces. Stuart, the Bronx Zoo field scientist stationed in Venezuela, met us with a broad smile on his ruddy face. He could see the look of dismay on my face.

"We need protection in this place, even when the locals aren't rioting," he said casually, as if everyone needed to live that way, or riots were a daily occurrence.

My mind refused to acknowledge the distant shots, clearly audible to anyone with ears. I had come to arrange something so life-affirming—saving priceless ecosystems with like-minded international colleagues, but now I felt sick and confused. I could not return to New York without firm plans in place, since a couple of hundred conference participants were depending on me.

After Stu, as he liked to be called, showed us around his spacious hacienda and introduced us to his wife and their two blonde little girls, we caucused about how to deal with the surreal circumstances.

"You'll just have to wait this out," he said, handing me another drink.

"But where?" I asked.

Surely, we couldn't stay here, so close to the mayhem on the streets.

"Don't worry, I'll get an experienced driver to take you to Rancho Grande tomorrow, and I'll meet you there in a day or two."

As the afternoon melted into darkness, the shooting accelerated, so it was no longer isolated pops. We stood at Stu's living room window overlooking a valley and watched the explosions light up the night sky one after another.

"This has sure escalated from tire burning," David said, and told Stu about the scenes we had witnessed earlier in the day in city center.

"Well, if they hadn't all been driving these giant gas guzzlers maybe folks would be less upset." Stu replied, but his voice trailed off.

I could see he was as distraught as we were, and he wasn't leaving in a week. He lived here.

"I wonder if these are warning shots, or if anyone is getting killed," I said.

"I'll get tomorrow's paper, then we might know, but don't count on it. Truth is elusive here," he said.

Just then the front gate buzzer went off, a shrill sound competing with the shots in the valley.

"I wonder who is coming this late?" Stu approached the monitor to see.

"Oh, its Dr. Fuentes, my next-door neighbor."

He buzzed him in to the frantic barking of dogs.

Dr. Fuentes, a small gray-haired gentleman, entered the living room with an anxious look on his weathered face. "Bad evening at the hospital," he said, "So many wounded and worse... " His voice trailed off.

"We've just been speculating about that. How about a drink?" Stu asked.

"Make it a stiff one. By my estimate, between our casualties and other area hospitals, at least 300 were killed today."

Now it was real.

"The working stiffs won't be able to afford gasoline if the subsidies aren't restored," Stu said. "How many will have to die for things to change?"

"Yes, and the poorer folks will starve," Dr. Fuentes added.

◆◆◆

Next morning, we sped along to the Henri Pittier National Park. Even as far back as the 1940s, Dr. William Beebe, the New York Zoological Society's preeminent head of the Department of Tropical Research, had studied the rich fauna of the cloud forest in this park, a magnet for scientists from around the world. The driver, instructed to take side roads and avoid any streets around the university, seemed rightfully preoccupied with dodging bullets. He was not in a conversational mood, but we did discover that the ride would last three hours if we were lucky.

It felt eerie to be driving through neighborhoods I'd have loved to explore on foot in other circumstances, and even worse when we passed the slum areas with shacks teetering on hillsides, ready to tumble into the trash-filled valleys below. At regular intervals police stood with rifles at the ready to shoot any looters. A national emergency had been declared, a curfew imposed, and all constitutional rights suspended. I felt as if I were back in the communist Poland of my youth, immersed in a bizarre dream.

Signs of the revolt subsided as we got closer to *Parque Nacional Henri Pittier*. Situated in the coastal mountain range, Venezuela's oldest protected area is a treasure trove of wildlife with well over 500 species of birds alone. The park's headquarters and biological station, *Rancho Grande*, turned out to be a sprawling and somewhat decaying concrete complex, built in the 1920s. Originally intended as a home for then-dictator Juan Vicente Gomez, the building was never fully completed, which added to its partially ruined look. Bats inhabited many of the empty rooms and others served as poorly-equipped dormitories. There were remnants of labs and ghostly offices and a sad-looking kitchen. I decided immediately that my conference participants couldn't stay here. Sure, I wanted them to enjoy the park's abundant wildlife, but I'd have them lodged in a more comfortable hotel.

At its lofty elevation, the park was cool and humid. Whoops of howler monkeys reverberated through the trees, adding to the unsettled feeling.

Given the curfew, even here away from the urban unrest, we headed to a hotel in the area after a short time in the park. Along the way, we passed a school where a small crowd of young people were gathered around a smoldering tire.

I was concerned about the entire situation and whether Stu would manage to get out of the city to meet us the next day. The hotel was modest and clean and I was relieved that it had an English news channel. We turned it on immediately, but the reception was so poor that it proved useless. I felt frustrated at my inability to understand the local news, but the images it showed disturbed us: bloody people running, smoke rising somewhere in the background, and angry groups chanting and waving placards.

"Let's go down to the bar," David suggested, "Maybe we'll get some more information there."

Among the patrons, a few expats nursed drinks and chatted about the events of the last two days. Speculations on the number of people killed by government troops in Caracas ranged from a few hundred to thousands. The news was horrifying, and it seemed especially in poor taste to speak so casually about these deaths in a bar. People were dying at the hands of their own government, simply for protesting! The repressive tactics made me feel sick, especially when I recalled the government repression in communist Poland that my family was lucky to escape. These poor people had nowhere to go. And then my thoughts turned to my reason for the visit. How will I ever do what I came for, and even more urgently, how will we ever get out of here? These questions made me queasy and my temples pounded until the *Cuba libres* took effect.

Still waiting for Stu to arrive the next morning, we decided to visit a nearby butterfly farm. It wasn't clear whether it would be open, in light of the national emergency, but we decided to try. The driver knew exactly where it was, tucked in a remote mountainous cul-de-sac—we'd have never found it ourselves. The owner, a young bearded man, short of stature, greeted us with an enormous grin: "*Visitantes! Un que placer! Soy Ramon,*" he called out as we rolled down the windows and pulled in on the unpaved road. Ramon must have seen we were gringos, as he then said in English, "You can park right here, next to my wife's Buick."

He pointed to a whale of vehicle with a rusting fender. "How would they afford the new astronomical gas prices?" I wondered. As I stepped out of our car he approached, stuck out his hand and shook mine enthusiastically.

Dusty toes sticking out of his brown leather sandals and a loose white guayabera shirt made him look like a hippie. It turned out that he held a doctorate in entomology from Cornell University and he had started his butterfly business only recently. His young wife worked as a teacher quite some distance away, to support the family and the butterflies. The remote location was a mixed blessing: too few paying visitors, but a safe, relatively undisturbed area for his exceptional collection.

Ramon bubbled with excitement about his colorfully winged insects. He explained each of the butterflies that alighted on our arms and heads—one more beautiful than the next. The iridescent blue morphos were the most dramatic. "Can you believe that people kill them to make pictures and jewelry using their wings?" Ramon asked.

"Yes, I know. Ugh, how can anyone want them dead, or wear them?"

There were dozens swirling in a blue haze. It made me happy they were protected here.

"Look at this pink-cheeked cattleheart!" Ramon exclaimed.

The butterfly sat on David's shoulder while I observed closely, trying to discern the accuracy of its name.

"Ramon, what is this one?" I turned to the elegant butterfly that stood out starkly against his white sleeve.

"That's a red-sided swallowtail," he said proudly.

"It looks like a woman dressed in a little black dress with a delicate ruby necklace—just a touch of color for drama," I said.

"You must like fashion," he said. "But it may surprise you that when this kind is a caterpillar, it is blue and yellow, with white stripes."

Ramon's steady stream of explanations created a kind of music in this enchanted place. It was the perfect refuge from the mayhem unfolding in the cities. I was moved by this man, so dedicated to protecting his stunning aerial jewels that creating the best ecosystem for them far surpassed the alarming reality of current events. The country was sliding into chaos, but all Ramon could think about were his butterflies.

"Without visitors like you and your upcoming conference, we'd have a much tougher time protecting them," he said, like a proud father.

"You know about *my* conference?" I could hardly conceal my surprise.

"Sure do. Everybody who is anybody in the environmental education field is planning to come. I'll be submitting a paper myself."

"So, I have the pleasure of meeting my first conference participant!"

This was exciting, but my angst about getting back to Caracas and making all the arrangements returned to the fore. I tried to concentrate on what he was saying, but the conference details swirled in my head: keynote speakers, panelists, hotel rooms, conference venue, audiovisual equipment, printing facilities for the proceedings, field visits, and even visas for some developing country attendees. Several hundred people were depending on me. I thought my brain would explode.

On our return to the hotel, we found Stu, who described his trip out of the city where the shooting was accelerating hour by hour.

"No way we can get back there now," he said definitively. "I'm here to make sure you dig in for a few days until things calm down a bit."

"So, what shall we do?" I was totally exasperated.

"This hotel has the best bar around for miles, and wait till you taste the beef in their restaurant," Stu gestured toward the stand holding the menu. "Their *churrasco* is to die for," he smacked his lips.

"This may not be as bad as you think, Annette," David said, "*Cuba libres* and slabs of prime Venezuelan beef, that's the life!"

"And don't forget the coffee, smooth and rich—the best in South America," Stu got into the act of cheering me up.

All I managed was a wan smile.

◆ ◆ ◆

Four days passed, enhanced by pounds of beef to clog all my arteries and enough rum to last a lifetime. Daily treks through the park—with spider monkeys cavorting in the canopy; tapirs rustling below, and the sounds of a hundred exotic birds I couldn't identify—calmed my nerves a bit. But on the fourth day I said, "Enough of this! If I can't go in person to see all the venues, let us try as best we can to reach all the points of contact by phone." I knew I had to begin to organize now, even if we couldn't get back to Caracas. Luckily, Stu agreed and helped translate numerous multi-party phone calls.

A week passed, and it was time to return to New York. I had done a reasonable amount of preparatory work under less-than-ideal conditions and hoped to smooth out any rough edges later. We still had little information about the state of the civil unrest in Caracas, but Stu, ever the resourceful scientist, had an idea.

"Let me make sure it's OK for you to get on the road to the airport," he said.

He went into a room to make a private call.

"It's alright, you can go," he said "But be cautious, keep your head down. There are snipers on rooftops."

"What?"

"Yes, do what I'm telling you," he said, turning serious.

"Who did you call?" I asked.

"The CIA," he said, "We are equipped with the contact numbers. It's a necessity here," he said, and I didn't want to know any more.

I swallowed hard and we said our goodbyes.

On the drive back, we heard more gunshots in the distance and saw crowds gathered on the streets, but things seemed calmer overall and we managed to get to the airport without any confrontations.

◆◆◆

On my return, the CEO greeted me, "What's this I hear? You arrive in a perfectly stable country and a revolution begins. It ends the day you leave. Any explanations?"

"You have to shake things up once in a while to get things done," I smiled.

Later I asked colleagues what *The New York Times* had reported on what Venezuelans at the time called—*Caracazoo*—The Big One! "I read that over 300 people were shot on the streets of Caracas; we really worried about you," one colleague told me.

In 1990, my conference succeeded beyond wildest expectations: 230 educators and scientists from 22 countries attended the gathering in a peaceful, vibrant Caracas I had missed on my first visit. And the networks that we developed then still continue today.

It wasn't until 2011 that the 3,000 victims of those bloody clashes between citizens and their government were acknowledged, ten times the number originally reported. Seventy-one of the bodies that had been hastily dumped in anonymous graves were exhumed and reburied in a marble pantheon to their memory. Hugo Chavez called the event a "massacre," and this time it was not hyperbole.

So many tragedies, human and animal, and yet at the same time, my heart had been filled with those stunning butterflies.

CHAPTER 20

Definitely Not Ordinary

People like to poke fun at the human-like behaviors of our nearest kin—monkeys and apes—to disguise the discomfort they often feel when watching them. Our fascination with the similarities between us is the reason why primate exhibits are among the most popular in zoos. My office in the venerable Heads and Horns building was very close to the Monkey House, and I rarely missed an opportunity to walk through it on my way to meetings or to lunch. In part, my stopovers had something to do with my job—interpreting animal life to the lay public—but I mostly went because I was as mesmerized as everyone else by their curious human-like antics. Of the several species on exhibit there were three that kept me glued, spellbound, and observing for long periods.

One of my favorite simian species was the capuchin monkey, which lived in a large social group dominated by a single alpha male. I often thought about their singularly inappropriate name. Early South American explorers named them after Capuchin friars who wore brown hooded robes, but to me they did not resemble friars in the least. The first observers were clearly not familiar with Orthodox Jews. Looking straight at the pink faces of the capuchins, I always saw *kippahs*, or *yarmulkas*—the skullcaps worn by Orthodox men. Not only did I see the skullcaps clear as day, so did my colleague Ann, and we came to call the monkeys our Jewish friends.

"*Shalom*, how are you today?" we'd say as we stopped to see what they were up to. Invariably, the youngest members of the group would be scampering about, chasing one another like yeshiva boys on a break from their studies. Mothers sat demurely cuddling their newborns and watching the youngsters at play. Sometimes when an older juvenile grabbed the tail of a younger one, the mother would swat him as if to say, "Leave your brother alone." The father usually sat on the highest branch calmly looking over his tribe, yet always ready to intervene if a fight broke out.

Looking at the busy scene, Ann and I often remarked about the incredible intelligence of these monkeys. In the wild they had been observed cracking palm nuts by placing them on an indented hard surface to keep the nut from rolling away and then cracking it with a larger nut or a stone brought from as far as a mile away. Research had shown that they could identify the faces of their relatives from photographs, and there were reports of captive individuals whose paintings resembled those of Andy Warhol's. The most intriguing bit of research showed that they could exchange coins for food and seemed to select offerings based on price. There was so much more to these animals than their ingenious antics!

Another exhibit in the Monkey House attracted attention, but for a different reason. The Proboscis monkeys, with their military crew cuts and long pendulous noses, were living caricatures of Jimmy Durante, and their behavior was even more shocking to visitors than their faces. These social animals, exhibited as a group, were dominated by a remarkable male whose stern gaze and huge canines would always stop mischievous youngsters in their tracks. But it was the sexual behavior of this male that shocked and attracted the most attention. He would demonstrate his supremacy by displaying, below what looked like a beer belly, a bright red erect penis, which he rubbed with obvious pleasure.

Teachers approaching the exhibit would glance in horror and shoo away their class groups, calling, "We are late for the bus! Let's go! Let's go!" Mothers with young children didn't have that option and often stood mortified while the child would comment, "Look, mommy, he has a booboo on his peepee."

"Do you want to see the tigers?" was most often an effective distraction. For teenagers passing the Proboscis exhibit, the sight was a cause for titters and quick knowing glances. I knew they would have laughed had they known that it was the fleshy nose magnifying the male's call in the wild that was *the* feature designed to attract females. The females, too, were a sight to behold with their small perky upturned noses, an amusing contrast to the males.

Had they been better observers, the visitors might have seen more interesting parts of their anatomy—the webbed hands and feet that allow these champion swimmers to get away from crocodiles, their most dangerous predators on the island of Borneo. Maybe, with my science training and daily opportunities to observe animals, I had more experience to spot these amazing adaptations. I suppose it wasn't fair of me to expect the same of casual visitors, but I knew that the very survival of these animals depended on the public's appreciation.

♦♦♦

I don't know if the search for the uncommon is a general human attribute, or one specifically belonging to Americans. We seem to always strive for something that stands out, something that is exceptional and the opposite of common: hotels like The Grand Del Mar or the Golden Strand, watering holes like the Emerald Lounge, or even the American Express Platinum card. In the animal world, many birds are blessed with grandiose names too: the great argus pheasant, the elegant crested tinamou (mountain hen), the golden pheasant, the fairy penguin, or the resplendent quetzal, Guatemala's national bird. And yet in my line of work I came across several species that were stuck with the unwelcome label of *common*. Many birds suffer with this demeaning moniker: common merganser, common teal, common shelduck, common kestrel, to name just a few. And even the stunning red panda is called a "lesser" panda. Who comes up with these insulting names? I wonder if, as result, these species are considered less important. If it were up to me, we'd stick with the scientific naming scheme developed by Carl Linnaeus in the eighteenth century; most people wouldn't understand the insults if they were in Latin.

The marmoset exhibit always attracted crowds because those lively little primates can hijack one's attention for longer than, say, an exhibit of exotic deer. Although the Monkey House itself was built at the turn of the century and was outdated by modern standards, each spring and summer I heard the roar of the crowds heading into the building.

Stopping by the marmoset exhibit to get my fix of animal-watching became a habit. I was most captivated by their tiny lively faces and foreheads endowed with a white blaze, and white tufts of fur on the sides of their heads that gave them a royal appearance. Their eight-inch bodies were covered in soft grayish-brown fur, and though their foot-long bushy tails made them seem larger, they were the smallest primates in the building.

Ann and I had a special mission that we carried out on fall days when heavy rains turned the grassy areas of our campus into swamps. On those days, the building stood all but empty, and we enjoyed its warmth and quiet, undeterred by its smelly aroma. It was a welcome respite from the throngs of summer and the piles of paper on my desk. We'd stop in front of the glass wall that separated us, watch their antics for a while, then, with a nod to their ID label: *common marmoset*, we'd allow ourselves the illicit luxury of anthropomorphism and tell them, "You are not common, not common at all." Some would come close to the glass and tilt their little animated faces at us, trying to figure out what these odd women were doing. But we'd insist on giving them their dose of therapy for self-respect, "No, no, no. You are *definitely* not common. You are special." It was a good thing no visitors were around. They might have thought we were crazy.

But really, all a smart human needed to do was to consider the highly-evolved behavior of these simians to know they were anything but common. Marmosets surpass many humans in their social structure. How many human fathers, for example, can say they have toted their twins non-stop for two weeks after their birth to take the burden off their tired momma? Marmosets usually give birth to twins; tiny one-ounce babies that grab onto the daddy's back to be carried right away. But fathers aren't the only family members that help. Aunts and sisters and other females in the group pitch in as well. In this primate society, "It takes a village to raise a child" is taken with seriousness. They practice cooperative infant care as a matter of routine. How else would these little helpless monkeys survive in the forests of Brazil, scampering along, unprotected from arboreal snakes, raptors, and wild cats?

And if child-rearing methods aren't impressive enough, consider their male-female relationships. Marmosets are generally monogamous, with only occasional lapses. Males in the group do not mate with closely-related females and know they must keep their distance. And if eating habits are any indication of style and class, consider the marmoset diet of bird eggs, fruits, flowers, and the occasional spider: pretty sophisticated and slimming.

Not common at all.

CHAPTER 21

China Redux

D r. George Schaller, the Derek Jeter of field biology, stuck his head into my office. I could hardly believe he was here in the Bronx, in the flesh. George was never around. Most of his time was spent in the wild: the remote rainforests of the Congo, the grasslands of Tanzania, or the lonely plateaus of Tibet. I looked at his trim, tanned figure, thinking he cut the perfect image for a Rolex ad. Although George was a field scientist, he showed considerable interest in what was going on at the Zoo. This made him a rarity among the field scientists.

"Hi Annette," he said, in an accent tinged with his native German, "I gave your *Pablo Python* and *Survival Strategies* courses to my Chinese colleagues in Yunnan."

I looked at him, incredulous and immensely impressed. How did he know about these materials? We had been working on them for several years, perfecting them and evaluating their use in hundreds of U.S. schools, but there was little dialogue between educators and scientists.

"But George, they won't be able to use them without instruction. They require extensive teacher training and preparation. And besides, most of our examples are American species."

"But I heard that your materials were so well-received in Belize. They love them over there," he said.

"That is so nice to hear, George." I blushed. My face must have been the color of a pink-faced bald uakari. The scientists rarely had much use for educators. "But they speak English in Belize, so at least we didn't have that hurdle," I said.

"Oh, I see." He raised his eyebrows and reached into his pocket.

"Here is the contact information in China, one of these folks speaks English reasonably well. Why don't you reach out? See what can be done."

With that he walked out, not to be seen again for many months, like the elusive cats he studied.

I stared at the card. It was in English on one side and Chinese on the other: Kunming Institute of Zoology, a branch of the Chinese Academy of Sciences. The memories of my trip a decade before came rushing back. I could clearly see the Kunming area landmarks: the Stone Forest, the flower and bird market, and Green Lake Park. The idea that our curriculum materials, designed for American classrooms, would work successfully in China seemed like a long shot, but the idea was intriguing.

I considered the pros and cons. China's wildlife was quickly losing ground to the burgeoning human population. Pandas,

South China tigers, freshwater dolphins, Yangtze alligators, and many bird species were under threat. If we could place our curricula in the schools and influence an entire generation of young Chinese to care for wildlife and wild places... what a dream. I must be nuts even to consider it. Chinese authorities must be like Cerberus, the Hound of Hades, guarding their curricula from anything Western that can poison young minds. They'd never let us in. Still... what if?

I glanced at my watch and calculated what time I'd have to call Kunming to speak with Dr. Ji. The 12-hour difference meant I'd have to place the call from home in the evening. All day long the idea tickled my brain. What if? What if? Whose backing would we need to make inroads into the formal school system? How would we translate the books, the discovery cards, the teachers' manuals? Could we revise them to include more Chinese species? Make the games more culturally relevant? The obstacles mounted the more I thought about George's suggestion, but the notion that he had carried the heavy boxes of materials all the way to China, and that he thought it worthwhile, had to count for something.

And praise coming from George Schaller, the man whose studies of mountain gorillas, lions, and pandas shook the scientific world... that was something. If he thought it could work, well, maybe it could.

♦ ♦ ♦

Dr. Ji was the senior scientist and director of the Kunming Institute of Zoology. His voice, coming across the thousands of miles, interrupted by buzzing and pinging, sounded very enthusiastic.

"When can you come here? I'll set up a meeting with the Yunnan Education Commission. You'll tell them why they should use your *Babalou* program and the other one too."

What is he talking about? It didn't make sense.

"Excuse me Dr. Ji, which program?"

"You know the one with the snake on the cover."

"Oh, yes, I see," I realized that it was a pronunciation thing.

Babalou was Pablo, our python mascot who leads the scientific expedition!

◆◆◆

Several weeks later I found myself in Kunming, sitting in a huge conference room lined on all sides by overstuffed chairs whose bulky arms were adorned with delicate white-crocheted doilies. More than a dozen serious-looking Chinese officials in navy-and-green Mao jackets sat staring at me solemnly. In front of each chair was a low table, set with a lidded china tea mug and a pot of green tea. The directors of various units within the Yunnan Education Commission had gathered to listen to my outrageous proposal that a Western-made curriculum be adopted by their schools. Dr. Ji, tall and slender, whose youthful face belied his years of experience surviving the Cultural Revolution, served as my interpreter. His regal bearing suggested a man savvy in dealing with the system.

"Thank you for your warm welcome, colleagues," I began. "I'm glad I made it across the street with the river of bicycles."

Some titters filled the room immediately; clearly, a few of them knew English. Then Dr. Ji translated to more laughter, and the ice had been broken. I explained my reason for creating these unusual curricula and their success in U.S. schools. By then the programs for elementary and middle school students were being used in 25 states. What made these programs different was that they engaged children's natural interest in animals to help them think about broader questions of biology, ecology, and wildlife survival. Most of all, it was science learning based on fun, but it depended on teachers giving up some control and allowing the students to take the lead.

To my great surprise, the administrators were most interested in our program's teaching techniques. They asked lots of questions and made surprising comments.

"We have become too accustomed to the teacher standing at the front of the room, being the giver of all wisdom," said one gray-haired gentlemen with a deeply-lined face.

His statement seemed to question authority, and I wondered how he managed to survive in a regime expecting everyone to toe the line. Was he thinking of the Communist party bosses giving the nation of over a billion rules to live by? This one's a rebel at heart, I thought.

It turned out that this man was instrumental in guiding the Commission in reaching a decision a week later—a definite "maybe."

"We won't be able to inject your curricula into our Yunnan province schools willy nilly. It'll take some work," Dr. Ji said. He explained that the Commission would require a one-year period of evaluation to study our curricula. Then, if they found them appropriate, they'd translate them into Chinese and print the Chinese editions.

"And what about approval from Beijing?" I asked Dr. Ji, because I knew nothing was ever done without a nod from the central government.

His response was an enigmatic smile followed by, "Yunnan is very far from Beijing. We have our own notions of… " he did not complete the sentence and I knew not to push further.

Amazed that I had gotten this far, I returned home, hopeful but not convinced that a year hence we'd have an affirmative response from the Commission. The Chinese were waking up to environmental issues, and that strengthened my belief that we might be welcomed. At least the authorities were willing to discuss things this time around, unlike the man who had barred our group from entering the panda reserve on my last trip to China.

♦ ♦ ♦

A year later, almost exactly to the day, I returned to China for the historic training sessions with Ann, our top-notch trainer, whose unconventional techniques have endeared her to legions of teachers. My husband David came along on the trip to photograph the events, and we were also joined by an Aussie environmental educator based in China. The Yunnan Education Commission had translated the materials into Chinese, and we had suggested many examples of Chinese animal species for them to substitute in the lessons. Together, we had adapted the activities to better fit Chinese culture. The

Commission had selected schools in the remotest and poorest sections of the province for the first wave of trainings. We'd have to trek to a village in southeast Yunnan, on the edge of the rainforest in the Mekong river delta. I had no clue of what to expect, I only knew that U.S. soldiers had battled the Vietcong just on the other side of the border in Vietnam.

Two drivers, provided by the Institute to take care of us, drove us for hours over poorly paved roads. Each time we made a rest stop, they cautioned us to be careful in the outhouses.

"Don't step where the wood is rotten, too many people here have died drowning in excrement," they cautioned.

Well, now I knew we were out of the area that proudly announced on a banner, "Tourist Exploitation Area." Exploration, exploitation... to the Chinese ear it was all the same.

There were no Western tourists at our destination. That was made clear by the decrepit-looking cement building with broken windows and a non-functional elevator. The lone employee escorted us to the third-floor room. To my relief, I noticed a private toilet, but my happiness did not last.

The woman pointed toward it and said, "Peepee, no poopoo!"

I turned to the driver who had accompanied us to see the room.

"So where do we...?"

He simply pointed to the outhouse, three floors below. In short order I noticed the broken window in our room and wondered how we'd defend ourselves from the bird-sized tropical mosquitoes.

He saw me looking at it and said, "I may have some insect repellent in the car. Don't worry, tomorrow will be a nicer hotel."

The bathroom had no towels, and the driver advised us to walk down the one-block main street, a kind euphemism for "Go buy some." It was evening by the time we went out, accompanied by the drivers, whose job was to check the kitchen of each potential eatery to see if it was reasonably clean and if the water was truly boiled.

The street was one muddy unpaved lane, with what seemed like most of the village residents congregating on it, sipping tea out of Mason jars, squatting on the side of the road, or sitting on plastic chairs next to folding tables lit by lanterns. Ducks and chickens paraded in between the legs of chairs, tables, and people. The eerie sight was made stranger by the biggest attraction of all: an outdoor pool table looming at the end of the block. Obviously, in this one-diversion village, it served as a magnet for the youth.

We bought two towels from a small stand that sold candies and cigarettes, odd packets of toothpowder, and plastic bags. Each towel was not much longer than a washcloth, but much thinner, more like a dishrag really, but we were relieved that there was a shower in our future. Our purchase completed, we joined the pool game to the astonishment of the locals. Ann, a bit of a shark, passed as a champion to the cheers of the kids. It was heartwarming that the language of sports broke the ice. I knew that these kids, thirsty for anything new, would be a pleasure to teach.

In the morning, we followed a schedule prepared for us by our hosts: a tour of the rainforest, visits to local schools to meet with principals, followed by an evening banquet with local officials. The rainforest was the strangest of these experiences, though each could have competed for that honor. Walking through it, we did not hear a single bird chirp or any small mammal rustle in the canopy. The quiet was deafening. It was all too clear that anything alive in this forest has been hunted out of existence. Then we heard a loud crash that sounded especially disturbing in this ghostly forest. Our guides told us of a pair of elephants roaming here, semi-wild. They were rounded up each evening and chained in a small corral.

Walking up the hill, we saw a two-room schoolhouse with mere openings where windows should have been and its door wide open.

"It's so quiet. Are there any children in it?" I asked.

"Of course," the guide smiled.

We entered the room, where about 60 fourth- and fifth-graders were bent over math exercise books doing work. There was no teacher anywhere in sight.

"What happened to the teacher," I asked.

"She is sick today. The children are working on their assignments, as you can see."

I was speechless. Five dozen children doing their work without any supervision! I picked up the notebook of a boy whose impish smile and mischievous eyes I could not resist. His math problems were all neatly written and all correct. I gave him the universal thumbs-up sign to titters from the rest of his classmates. So, these kids were self-starters! The perfect subjects for our programs. I felt like we had come to just the right place.

But the evening banquet brought totally unexpected challenges that had nothing to do with the appropriateness of our programs. My Chinese hosts toasted me repeatedly with glasses of *maotai*, the traditional alcoholic drink made of fermented sorghum. After all, I was a senior American official. I knew that to refuse the toasts would insult them, but drinking the 53% alcohol liquor would rot my gut and make me a laughing stock by end of the evening.

This is where David's presence was a life-saver: he saved my reputation while risking his. Surreptitiously, I snuck each drink to him, when it seemed my hosts wouldn't notice. In between the toasts, an endless variety of dishes graced the table, none of which I could identify, except for delectable purple rice served inside a pineapple. At the beginning of the meal I asked Dr. Ji what we were eating, but all he would say was, "It's good for your health," with a cryptic smile, so I gave up asking. Luckily, the one *maotai* that actually reached my stomach had clouded my mind, so I didn't dwell on the images of skinned dogs we had seen at the food market or the other less-identifiable carcasses we had seen hosting all of the neighborhood flies.

As our drivers had promised, the following night we moved still closer to the Mekong River, where the actual training session would be held. This was a homier accommodation, but we arrived in the dark. After disembarking from the vehicle, the four of us—me, Ann, David, and the Aussie—followed our drivers single-file along a narrow path surrounded on each side by grasses taller than our heads. "Darn it! I wish I hadn't buried the flashlight at the bottom of my backpack," I thought, as squishy sounds underfoot competed with the buzzing of mosquitoes overhead. We walked in silence for what seemed like a mile. Where are they taking us? I wondered.

Momentarily losing sight of the man I was following, I heard a chortle—a cross between a laugh and a scream. Soon enough, I understood why. We had to cross a rickety swinging bridge made of wooden slats that were spaced too far apart for comfort.

"Don't worry, we'll be OK," I shouted to the companions behind me, my heart in my stomach and my eyes straining to make out what was ahead.

Eventually, we were escorted up a wooden staircase to a house perched on stilts over water, though we could not discern its depth in the dark. Only the gentle sloshing below gave us a clue. Inside, which was nearly as dark as outside, we walked through different rooms, finally arriving in a space that glowed pink.

"Where are we? Is this a brothel?" Ann exclaimed, and all of us burst out laughing in the dark. The driver lit a candle and we saw the beds swaddled in swirls of pink mosquito netting.

"See, I told you this would be a nicer hotel," the driver said, grinning.

The odd shadows danced on the wall at his back.

♦ ♦ ♦

The training workshops over the next several days went off without a hitch and we were all amazed at how similar the participants were to Western teachers—taking notes, eagerly scooping up worksheets and handouts—but with one exception. They were very reluctant to ask questions, something we tried to encourage. After much prodding, we discovered that in their culture asking questions signifies a failure on the instructor's part to explain things clearly. We ensured them that we welcomed all questions, and Ann loosened up the group by playing her guitar. We taught them American songs, and they tried to teach us Chinese songs. They were clearly the better students.

As with the Belize educators, by the end of the sessions we parted as friends, promising to return within a year to see how things worked out in real classrooms. I even managed to say *shie, shie* and *zay jian* ("thank you" and "good bye"), when we left.

◆◆◆

True to our promise, we returned a year later. It would be difficult for anyone who did not witness it in person to understand just how skillfully the Chinese instructors were teaching the lessons, with classes averaging 50 to 60 students. We watched in stunned silence as the children carried out complex experiments and simulations. The principals gave us glowing reports of student progress. They also told us how much the parents appreciated their children's new interests. Best of all, word of our program's success had reached Beijing!

Unexpectedly, instead of a rebuke, the Yunnan Provincial officials received praise for their innovation and the doors opened wide for my subsequent negotiations with China's Minister of Education to expand the programs to many more schools.

The day George Schaller stuck his head in my office had opened the floodgates. It wasn't long before our trainers were headed for Papua New Guinea, Thailand, India, Cuba, and elsewhere, bringing *Babalou* and his mates to classrooms in corners of the world where wildlife needed not only protection, but new generations of supporters. Our work made it possible for thousands of students to develop a new appreciation for the natural world. Or as Pablo would say, "Hey, kids, join me on an adventure of a lifetime!"

CHAPTER 22

The Fugitive

David and I spotted it from the distance as we drove down a steep hill on Hewins Street amid the lush farmland of Sheffield, Massachusetts. A large animal raced down the hill in front of us, but it was too far away and we couldn't quite tell what it was. Too short to be a deer or a cow, too squat and broad to be a large dog, it perplexed us.

"What the… ?" I said. "David, speed up so we can get a better look."

As we got closer, we were astounded to see a runaway hog. He must have weighed at least 400 pounds and was amazingly agile on his short legs. Then it dawned on us: the Fourth of July barbecues would be fired up the next day. This guy must have escaped a sorry fate, and we were not about to alert any of the nearby farmers. We laughed and cheered him on. Then, I remembered…

At the zoo, I always knew when spring arrived, and it wasn't by looking out the window. After my first office that looked out on the elk enclosure, I spent years in a window-less office and unconsciously learned to interpret the outside world by signals that weren't visual, much like animal adaptation. On this day, excited shouts, peals of laughter, and giggles bubbling out of the mouths of kindergarteners were the signal that we were past Easter. The predictability of seasonal change felt comforting, but oddly, it also made me think that too much routine can be numbing. Maybe I just needed a vacation, a chance to run free on a beach somewhere.

A group of schoolchildren had gathered in the lobby of my building, waiting for their tour guide. The massive, exterior carved doors to the building were open and more noise, carried on gusts of mild air, blew toward my inner sanctum each time someone opened the glass doors leading from the lobby to the Education offices. Every April brought hundreds of school groups, released from their stuffy classrooms to taste more of the freedom that had been doled out in miserly minutes during winter recess. Enticed by the sounds, I walked out of my office, leaving behind my thick sweater. It was so bright I wished I'd remembered my sunglasses.

Classes were lined up outside the building in varied states of orderliness. Some had class clowns gesticulating wildly, emulating the howler monkeys; others stood roughly in lines that were disrupted each time someone spotted a squirrel scampering about the grounds. "Look, look, they got out of the cage," they'd scream. Inner-city kids, I sighed, even squirrels were a sight.

I knew that guides would soon be leading them to the Children's Zoo to learn something about living creatures. For many of these children, mice, roaches and the occasional mutt or tabby were the only known representatives of the animal kingdom. I decided to follow the trail of laughter, noticing the irresistible fragrance of early spring honeysuckle.

The Children's Zoo buzzed with activity. There was so much to do and experience in the new exhibit that even the most placid youngsters became slightly wild, running from one activity to the next, wanting to do it all at once. The children could hardly wait to climb up the spider web, sit in a giant bird's nest, burrow in a log, or peek into the saguaro cactus that hid a surprise.

I was proud of these new exhibits and my part in their design, although planning the renovation had been fraught. As much as I respected tradition, I admit I was part of destroying a piece of it here. The original Children's Zoo was centered on nursery rhymes and biblical images of animals, because it had been designed in a different age. But in a modern, scientifically-based zoological garden, these kinds of representations of animals no longer served the zoo's goals. Back in the day, Noah's Ark depicted the noble concept of saving pairs of species. But now the zoo had a bigger mission: saving animals in their own habitats, so that those in zoos were not the only ones left. Noah's Ark used to dominate the center, and the kids did find it entertaining. When the subject came up, even David said, "Oh, don't take down the Ark, I used to love it when I was a boy."

But after much enlightening research on experiential learning, we decided to launch a major renovation: we would tear down the old exhibits and replace them with new ones that would allow children to physically experience how animals live: their habitats, behaviors, and diets. In the new design, Noah's Ark had to go, but the designers were careful to preserve the farmyard feature from the old design. The new plan included an area where children could pet the goats, feed the cows and chickens, and get up-close and personal with domestic animals that were as exotic to them as the most obscure wild species. Most of the visitors were much too young to remember the zoo's Noah's Ark, so they had no reason to miss it. But every now and then, an older visitor would ask for directions to the ark and wince in disappointment that it was gone.

The domestic petting area, by far the best part of the new Children's Zoo tour, was saved for last. As soon as they entered it, the children's biophilia, or innate tendency to connect to the natural world, was evident. They stretched their short arms out, reaching as far as they could to touch the coarse fur of the goats and the oily curls of the lambs. The brave ones held out their small palms, offering food pellets and squealing with joy when raspy, wet tongues swept the food up and looked for more.

The place reverberated with an unlikely choir of quacking, honking, mooing, and braying mixed with laughter and the occasional cries of someone who imagined their finger had been nipped by a greedy goat. But one day it was the grunting that attracted my attention most.

I knew that we exhibited piglets each spring who magically disappeared at the end of the season and seemed to return the following year, not a day older. But what I heard was not a piglet. It was a deep oink belonging to a mature pig. I approached the sound and my eyes fell on its hulking pink body sprawled in the dust. The pig had his eyes closed and something approaching a smile on his lips below an elongated snout, twitching in what I presumed was a sweet spring dream. The children around it were amazed by its sheer size. "Is it real?" they asked time and again. The keeper nearby said, "Yes, it's real. Can't you see him breathing? His name is Claude."

Now that he had a name, he evoked even more interest. The keeper was peppered with questions. "How much does he eat?" was the most urgent one.

"Well, I can tell you one thing, he sure is not a finicky eater," the keeper answered, and most of the children were satisfied, not caring to listen to a long, varied list of hog snacks. "How much does he weigh?" asked one of the parent chaperones.

"Oh, we haven't weighed Claude lately, but I bet he's at least 450 pounds," the keeper said with a chuckle.

I was also intrigued with Claude, because I knew that one season's piglets were next season's bacon. How had Claude managed to elude this fate? I wondered. I had no idea, and was quite curious about it, but it was time to get back to the office and face a desk full of "While You Were Out" pink message slips. I soon forgot my question about Claude.

♦ ♦ ♦

Eventually fall arrived with its delicious lessening of the crowds. The laughter of thousands of children became just an echo, and the Children's Zoo was closed for the season, another part of our seasonal routine. One day I needed to speak with a young woman who was the camel keeper and trainer. Now that the zoo paths were not packed with visitors, I could get into my electric cart and make it to the other end of our large campus in just a few minutes. I pulled into the back of the camel yard, an area closed to the public, and knocked on the camel barn door. A diminutive woman in knee-high rubber boots and a hose in one hand slid open the door.

"Hi, I was just cleaning up," she said, looking around the corner as if to check that I came alone. We spoke for a few moments about an ornery camel that refused to be trained for the camel rides, but she kept turning her head toward the gate in the yard I had left ajar.

"Want to see something?" she asked me suddenly.

"Sure, what?" I inquired with a slight sense that I was about to participate in something illicit.

"OK, but shut the gate first," she instructed. I did and she ushered me inside the camel barn where several of our dromedary camels were busy munching on hay. The barn was not well lit and I could not easily see everything in its darkened corners. "This way," she urged me. I turned the corner and there he was—Claude!

I gasped. He lay calmly on the straw, looking much larger than he had in the spring. Jeepers, he must be 600 pounds by now, I guesstimated.

"What in the world is he doing here?" I asked.

"Shh..." she said. "We're not supposed to keep him but look at him, isn't he wonderful? He was certainly remarkable, if not for his size alone, then for his illegal hideout. "We just couldn't give him up," she added, looking at me pleadingly, her eyes asking for agreement.

"Has he been here since last spring?" I asked, but the answer was obvious.

"Yes, we hide him from the director. Claude loves to hang out with the camels. He is so sociable and smart," she beamed. "He may be huge, but he's very sensitive."

"Does he ever go out?" I asked, still trying to process what I was seeing.

"In the summer, we let him lay out in the yard, but we had to slather him with sunscreen. His skin is very delicate, you know."

I smiled at this pink fugitive and the love he inspired, then I bent down and patted his flank. It was warm and its fuzz was surprisingly soft. Claude snorted in satisfaction. "How are you, big boy?" I asked.

He grunted.

"You found a great rest home with room service, didn't you?"

Another grunt. This was turning into a real conversation.

His sheer size and smug look made me think of the teacup piglets I had noticed some unscrupulous breeders advertising. I could just picture a pet lover buying Claude as a piglet and placing him in a cup, the kids and neighbors marveling at his petite sweetness. Then as he grew far larger than a small dog, ungainly and bereft of his cuteness, I imagined them bringing him to the zoo. How sad the children would be, how disappointed the owner, and what about the poor pig? An animal with so much intelligence would surely be upset. I knew that this was the fate of many miniature pigs, and was glad Claude had been given this most unconventional shelter.

"I've got to get back to the office," I said, climbing into my cart.

The keeper waved and put her finger to her lips.

"Thank you for taking me into your confidence and don't worry, I won't tell anyone," I called out as the cart rolled forward.

Only on the way back to the office did I realize that I had become an unwitting co-conspirator in a swine caper; and chuckled at this unexpected break in my routine.

CHAPTER 23

Carnivore's Delight

Kenya is one of those places that immediately bring to mind magnificent creatures: lions, rhinos, elephants, and leopards. It's a remarkable East African country, about the size of Texas, that straddles the equator. Despite its wilderness, its capital Nairobi is a bustling metropolis. Sadly, only a small population of Kenyans has the resources and opportunity to venture into the wild areas that surround the city. My zoo had been working with African governments for decades, setting up wildlife reserves and protected areas, and stationing field biologists throughout Africa's wildest areas. From the critically endangered gorillas of Cameroon to the elephants of Gabon, the lions of Kenya, and dozens of other charismatic animals of Nigeria, Congo, Uganda, Zambia, and other remote countries, we were at the forefront.

But there was one area that lagged behind—the education of the native people, whose attitudes were key to protecting these species. I knew that sooner or later this need would become as obvious to wildlife area managers and zoo administrators as it was to me. And I could tell it was gaining in importance when someone had an inspired idea: to borrow the educational techniques and exhibition strategies from our Children's Zoo and transplant them into the Nairobi Wildlife Park. Our innovative exhibits— which let the children climb and play in animal habitats like our climbing spider web, a giant nest, or a log tunnel—had been extensively copied in the U.S., so why not make them available in a place where they could make an even greater difference?

In 1996, such an opportunity blew in, like an exciting hot wind from the Sahara. And so, twenty-four years after I began my zoo career, I would travel to Kenya with a team of exhibit designers and animal specialists.

Boy, was I ready!

Based on the success of my programs in the U.S. and abroad and their recognition by the American Association of Zoos and Aquariums, I had been promoted to a vice president position, rare for a woman in the zoo world. Though the title was a nice acknowledgement, what pleased me most is that the trustees and senior administrators recognized the importance of education in a way they hadn't before.

The Kenyan Wildlife Service had invited us to consult on educational programs and animal facilities for the Nairobi Safari Walk they were planning. When complete, the Safari Walk would serve more Kenyans than the number that visited *all* of the country's national parks *combined.* It boggled my mind to think that Kenyan children, the inheritors of the world's spectacular wildlife heritage, had less opportunity to see giraffes, monkeys, and lions than New York city visitors to the Bronx Zoo.

As soon as we landed, I knew it was different from anywhere in the world I had been before—and I had lived on three continents. The air was thick and moist, suffused with dense smells I did not recognize. Was it human sweat mixed with fermented fruit? Sewage, or fire? The only familiar scent was the car exhaust, which wasn't very wild, but I hadn't yet arrived at our destination.

Our group of four piled into a van with squeaky springs. Slowly we meandered through thick urban traffic. This was nothing like the wild Africa I had imagined. I was captivated, though, by the sight of women in colorful cotton dresses, young and old, carrying large baskets on their heads, their feet bare and dusty. The driver told us about the city's mixture of ethnic groups, Kikuyu being the largest. While most faces were black, I could also see many white and Asian people in the crowds. The city was an odd mix of modern high-rise buildings, men in suits and ties, raggedy youths in torn T-shirts, and slums lined with rows of tightly-packed corrugated tin shacks on unpaved alleyways strewn with garbage.

As the city receded, each turn of the road brought me closer to the real Africa: open vistas and a sky larger and bluer than I had seen anywhere. We passed low buildings fronted by rickety stands of fruit; people squatting by the road waiting for the impossibly crowded buses; barefoot children running toward our van whenever we slowed down; donkey carts; jalopies sputtering exhaust; and large advertisements for Coca Cola plastered on roadside stands. Except for the occasional birds, we didn't see any big game animals yet. I couldn't wait to share these first impressions with David and the kids.

Eventually we reached the famed East African Rift Valley, the cradle of our civilization, where anthropologists discovered our hominid ancestors. This huge chasm, caused by shifting tectonic plates, is a vast area crossing twenty national borders. The small sliver of it I saw in Kenya will always be vivid in my mind for its vast ochre, tan, and green stretches dotted by grasses, whistling thornbush, sheep, and goats—all seemingly undisturbed by civilization. After four or five hours of driving, my back stiff from sitting in a cramped position, and exhausted from the long flight, I began thinking about our accommodations.

As I hadn't made the trip arrangements, I had no idea where we'd be staying, but as the city began to recede behind us, I knew it would be out of its immediate vicinity. Finally, the van pulled to the left onto a dusty road and it seemed we were headed into the heart of the savannah. "Is this where we are staying?" I asked our driver.

"Sure. Aren't you here to see the animals?" He smiled.

It was nearly sunset, I thought, not exactly a time for sightseeing, but all I said was, "Today?"

"Sure," he said again, but it wasn't clear what that meant.

Bumping along the dusty rutted road, we approached a round thatched-roof building. "You are at the reception," the driver announced, and jumped out of the van. There were no buildings anywhere in view. I began to feel anxious, but didn't want to let on to my three male companions—Lee, Mike, and Tim. This was Africa, after all, I couldn't be the weakest specie! Inside, a smartly dressed man in a white jacket offered us cold drinks on a tray. I lifted the glass with surprise and asked him, "Where is the hotel?"

"Hotel?" He looked at me strangely, then brightened. "You mean the tents?"

Tents? We are staying here in the middle of a wildlife park with lions, giraffes, warthogs, and wildebeest in *tent*s? I began to perspire. At first, I'd been worried about sharing close quarters with my male colleagues, but now I hoped they'd give us all a single large tent.

As soon as we registered, we climbed back into van and drove deeper into the savannah. It was getting dark, and except for the sea of gently swaying grass and distant acacia trees, not much was visible. Stopping in front of a tent, the driver turned to me and said, "Well, here it is." There was nothing as far as the eye could see, except for a few small flat-topped acacia trees in the distance.

"Are we all getting out here?" I asked.

"No. The guys have tents in a different part of the park. It's just you here," he said.

I'd be staying alone in a canvas tent in the middle of African wilderness! All alone! I hadn't counted on that when I'd happily accepted this assignment.

"Let me show you in and give you some pointers," the driver said.

A low wooden porch fronted the large square tent.

"Your butler will put out tea and breakfast on this porch for you early each morning." Butler? Room service? Here? I was too flabbergasted to speak. Then he led me inside and showed me the shower attached to the back of the tent, and instructed me on how to open the zippered windows if I wanted more air, and how to unravel the mosquito netting over what looked like a king size bed. A colorful wool rug covered most of the floor, giving the space unexpected elegance. I was too stunned to ask questions. All I could say as he was leaving was, "What about the animals?"

"Don't worry, they are here, all around. You'll hear the hyenas, but they won't bother you. We have guards with rifles on the periphery."

Rifles? Nearby hyenas? Lions? A shower in the tent? I could hardly absorb this. David will never believe this, I thought.

"Oh, I almost forgot," he said when he'd reached the porch. "The breakfast will be here at five tomorrow. We'll wake you so you can go on the walkabout before dawn." As he exited the tent, he called out, "Look for the present in your bed."

What does that mean? I wondered, but it was too late to ask because the van had pulled away, leaving behind a cloud of dust.

I took a luxurious hot shower, using the fragrant soaps provided in a soapstone dish carved with elephants. But how did they generate hot water here? Log fires? Solar units? Amazing. Feeling clean and somewhat relaxed I went to bed. Scooting under the linens, my toes touched something warm at the foot of the bed. I jumped, my heart in full fight-or-flight mode. I investigated cautiously: it was a hot water bottle! So, that's what he meant when he said I'd find a present. I calmed down, thinking that my kids would have been telling me not to jump out of my skin. It was getting quite cool and I realized the water bottle was meant to take the chill out of the sheets. I had never experienced such thoughtful service.

Lying curled up under warm blankets in a bed swathed in mosquito netting, I could not fall asleep. My mind raced with the impressions of our arrival. Then I began to listen to the sounds just outside my tent: strange coughing-like noises, barking, yips, low rumblings, loud snores, and finally the hyena howls. They sounded so near I was terrified. Eventually, I fell into a dreamless sleep only to wake up startled to noises on my tent porch. The breakfast! I remembered.

I reached for my khakis and long-sleeved safari shirt, then pulled on my hiking boots. I drank the hot tea eagerly, still unable to get over having room service in the wilderness. Soon the van arrived with my companions. We disembarked in the reception building, which was quite dark. A young Masai man introduced himself as our guide for the morning.

"Please sign these first," he said, distributing some small slips of papers.

It was much too early to read the tiny dense writing, and quite impossible to see what was written on them, but we all signed quickly and received instructions to walk as silently as possible behind the ranger.

We got on a path that meandered on grass moist with morning dew. It was dark and quiet except for distant calls of thrushes and insects buzzing. I found the rifle slung on the young ranger's shoulder reassuring. In his hand, he held a spear like a true Masai warrior. I recalled reading something about the danger of walking on foot in wilderness areas, but pushed the thought to the back of my mind. The ranger's voice was low and I listened intently to his every word. "Stay close and look at my hand signals." Gee, it's still too dark to see his hand signals, I thought. "And don't make any noises. Okay?" he asked, and just then Mike coughed. What about that? Was this kind of noise liable to provoke a predator? After about fifteen minutes, he motioned for us to stop and put a finger to his lips, indicating silence.

The ranger pointed ahead and not more than twenty feet from us a huge elephant cow (as females are called) stood, silently testing the morning air with her upraised trunk.

"Their sense of smell is better than a bloodhound's. She'll be able to smell us," he whispered. "Let's just stay here without moving a muscle."

Our little group shrunk into itself as we moved closer together. All we could hear was one another's breath.

"Look," the ranger whispered, "She's got a calf with her."

Indeed, a young elephant, about three feet tall, followed the female, turning his head in all directions, touching his mom with his trunk. I knew that elephant mothers are super vigilant when they have young in tow. Her hulking gray body towered about five feet above the baby, but every now and then she touched it tenderly with her trunk. She loomed so huge, I knew how easily she could have crushed us. We watched them for about ten minutes—as beautiful a natural sight as I've ever seen. Then they crossed our path majestically and moved on, leaving us in awe.

As we continued, the sun began to rise. The light and the pinkish sky made the vastness in front of us look primeval, magical. It seemed to go on forever, but I knew that such places are really like zoos, limited and encircled by human settlements. A giraffe ambled in the distance with its characteristic gait: two lefts, then two rights. She seemed to be floating above the earth. A zebra flashed by, then another, and another. I felt like I was in a PBS special. Our walk was coming to an end and I was grateful of one thing: that we hadn't run into a pride of lions or crocodiles. As we parted company from the ranger back at the reception building, I thanked him.

"So, for how many years have you been leading these fabulous bush walks?" I asked.

He smiled a radiant smile, showing his perfect white teeth, "Ma'am, I'm do this job four months," he said proudly.

I swallowed my gasp. And that's when it hit me: the papers we were asked to sign in the darkness were release slips. I later asked to see a copy and noted all the risks, from ticks to stings by malaria-bearing mosquitoes, bushfires, lightning, even death by black mamba, hippo, elephant, or Nile crocodile! Holy Jesus! I sure was glad it had been too dark to read it.

◆ ◆ ◆

After a long day of meetings with designers of the Nairobi Safari Park to discuss the plans, we returned tiredly to our camp. White tablecloths graced tables set out to face the park and the ambling antelope and gazelle, and cool drinks were waiting. We chatted and rested in the hammocks swinging between the few trees, watching red-tailed monkeys, mongoose, and the occasional wart hog strolling by. I was quickly falling in love with the place.

Next morning, we woke, raring to go out exploring the vast plain stretching before us, but this day we got our own jeep. We'd go into the wilderness alone, just us four American city folks! Tim got the keys only after we all heard the lengthy lecture from a ranger. First, he instructed us on what route to take for maximum wildlife viewing. And he concluded with, "Under no circumstances leave the vehicle. Understood?"

"Yes, boss," Tim saluted and jumped into the driver's seat.

We got on the road, bursting with anticipation. Soon, magnificent sights unfolded before us: herds of wildebeest, giraffes, zebra, and impala. These graceful animals ruled these plains. Each and every specie held me spellbound, but the giraffes were so gorgeous and dignified I held my breath each time they appeared in the bush, wrapping their long bluish tongues around acacia leaves and pulling down mouthfuls.

After a while we came to the Mara. This was the legendary river where dramas of life and death played out during annual migrations. I could hardly believe I was actually there. Wildebeest had to cross it, risking getting eaten by the crocodiles that lurked in the muddy waters or the lions who roamed nearby. We stopped to watch it flowing undisturbed, as it had for centuries. Almost immediately we spotted two enormous crocodiles, not ten feet from us. I snapped away too many camera shots to count, but I wanted a close-up my lens was unable to take, and I needed a better angle. Without thinking, I jumped off the vehicle to get closer, yet still remain safely out of their reach. I tiptoed forward. Lee stuck his head out of the jeep.

"Get back here! You heard what they told us. This is unsafe," he said.

"Come on, they are still as logs," I said and ignored him, focusing on my camera shots.

All at once I heard a strange hissing. It came from the vehicle. I turned and saw it emanated from Mike, who was gesticulating wildly but not uttering a word. He kept pointing to a nearby tree to the right of our jeep. I stared for a moment and saw nothing, but his hysterical waving told me something was wrong.

On second glance, I knew! A lioness and two cubs huddled next to the tree eyed me, their beige coloring blending perfectly with the savannah grasses.

I froze.

I didn't know if she would pounce if I moved toward the vehicle. Would it be best to stay still, as we had done with the elephant the day before? Or should I move cautiously and get into the jeep as soon as possible?

The thrill of being within a dozen feet of the king of beasts numbed my brain. I hardly realized I was potential juicy prey.

Instead of moving, I snapped a couple of shots, then without a sound, I shimmied back slowly into the vehicle, never taking my eyes off the lioness. Only when I plopped in the seat did I notice that my heart was about to fly out of my chest. I felt as if I was about to have a heart attack.

"Annette, Annette, are you okay?" my companions seemed concerned.

"I'm sorry," I mumbled, completely embarrassed by my stupidity. "I'll never, ever leave the safety of a vehicle again. I swear."

"Not even for a flat on the highway?" Tim teased me, breaking the tension.

◆◆◆

This was an exciting day of sightseeing, but that wasn't the purpose of our trip. Over the next week, we met with our African colleagues daily, discussing the pros and cons of various exhibit strategies, guided by our experience at the Bronx Zoo Children's Zoo. On the pro side: experiential learning is a more effective teaching tool. On the con side: the types of exhibits we had at the Bronx required a lot more supervision to avoid chaos and injury. We wanted Kenyan children to know the thrill of seeing Kenyan wild animals up-close, and imagined a sign that would say, *Children and Warthogs Have the Right of Way.*

On our last evening in Nairobi, our African partners invited us to join them in their favorite restaurant: Carnivore! The place was a large and raucous barbecue restaurant, modeled after the Brazilian *churrascarias.* Our group was settled at a large table by a jovial host who gave each of us a small flag. "Just raise this flag to signal you want more meat," he said. I am not much of a meat-eater, and my dining experiences in Belize and China made me even less so, so the idea of a meat extravaganza did not excite me. I hoped there would be plenty of vegetable selections at the buffet.

Our hosts ordered drinks and made curious quips about our virgin palates. I had no idea what they meant until a server showed up at our table holding a roasted hunk of meat on a spit.

"What is it?" I asked, dumbstruck by its size.

"A juicy shank."

I could not take my eyes off the four-foot sizzling hunk.

"From what animal?"

"Giraffe" he said.

My colleagues used their flags to indicate they wanted to try it. I shook my head to say I'd pass. I wanted to gag. Eating giraffe? Why, that's even worse than eating gibnut!

But this was just the beginning. A procession of waiters brought similarly impressive cuts of antelope, gazelle, crocodile, ostrich, zebra, wildebeest, even oryx. I was aghast. They were eating their natural heritage.

Not wanting to offend, I searched my mind for a delicate way to inquire about it. Seeing me pass every opportunity by keeping my flag down, they quickly figured out my problem and began to explain even before I asked.

"These animals are all ranched, like your cattle in the U.S.," they said. "It's perfectly all right to eat them. Try the giraffe, it's the best."

After I had turned down several of the game meats, I noticed our hosts getting increasingly uncomfortable, whispering to one another and casting glances my way. Maybe they were irritated with my refusals. I mustered my courage and tasted a slice of wildebeest. It must be similar to venison, I told myself, although I had never actually tasted deer meat. It turned out to be stringy and I made a polite, if unintelligible, comment when asked how it was.

Next came a chunk of crocodile. It was disgustingly gelatinous. I could neither swallow it nor spit it out gracefully. I excused myself and found a ladies' room to dispose of the morsel. When I came back they had piled two different portions of meat on my plate.

"Taste these and let us know which one you like better," they said, looking at me expectantly. OK, I'll do it for the honor of the Bronx Zoo, I thought, and lifted the fork to my mouth. The first piece tasted gamey, but I managed to swallow it.

"Now try the other," they urged.

The pressure was on. I took a chunk from the other side of the plate. It was juicy and pleasing, slightly sweet, like a good cut of steak marinated in a wine sauce. I smiled.

"This one is tasty," I said, and proceeded to eat the slices on my plate.

They applauded and I blushed.

"OK, now tell me what I just ate."

"The first piece was Thomson's gazelle; the second was giraffe."

Giraffe! I was horrified and speechless. All I could see were the giraffe's gorgeous eyelashes and its enchanting gait as it floated free on the savannah. I felt like a cannibal and couldn't wait for the evening to be over.

For years afterward, I kept the little flag to remind me of my crime. I was thrilled when I discovered eight years later that game meats had been banned in Kenyan restaurants. But I had toughed it out with the guys, and ultimately the Nairobi Safari walk would enchant thousands of Kenyan children in a safe, beautiful environment. They would see live giraffes.

CHAPTER 24

Mole Rats and Trustees

Now, someone unfamiliar with the politics and epic struggles that take place in elegant boardrooms might think that the keepers and curators and vets make a zoo what it is. Not quite.

At the venerable Bronx Zoo, one of the most famous in the world, the trustees are the cream of New York's high society, with no get-rich-quick schemers among them. Respectable old money ruled the zoo and had influenced its policies since its very founding. Had they not provided the funds, the vision, and the energy to buck City Hall at the end of the 19th century, this influential zoo might never have even been born.

What a loss that would have been to our fair city!

Laurance Rockefeller was one of those illustrious philanthropists whose vision, influence, and money protected hundreds of thousands of pristine acres teeming with wildlife in the Grand Tetons, and helped establish national parks like the National Redwoods Park in California, Haleakala National Park in Hawaii, and the Virgin Islands National Park. For over half a century, Rockefeller also contributed much in the way of funding and inspiration for the Bronx Zoo's exhibition and conservation efforts. Having served as chairman and president of the New York Zoological Society, as well as an advisor to five presidents on environmental and recreational policies, he was one powerful trustee. But he was not the only one. Some of New York's most eminent families could be found on the trustee roster at its inception, and are there still.

Since its founding in 1895, the zoo has grown in popularity so that today nearly a million people pour through its gates each year to see creatures they'd never be able to see in their native habitats: the savannahs of Africa, the jungles of South America, or the Asian steppes. The zoo's exhibitions open new worlds of wonder and inspiration for children and adults alike. Few people stop between exhibits to consider all the behind-the-scenes planning, curating, and political wrangling that goes into the city's greatest nature exhibitions, and the trustees are the most invisible individuals in this process. They are a subterranean society, with a hierarchy ruled by the chair of the board. Their power and money support the zoo and influence the development of new exhibitions.

By 1990, the zoo had many outstanding exhibitions—some of which were downright revolutionary, like The World of Birds, Wild Asia, the Carter Giraffe Building, JungleWorld, Himalayan Highlands, and the renovated Children's Zoo—and the trustees were now casting about for ideas for a new blockbuster. By this point in my career I had attended some of the board of trustees meetings, a rare privilege reserved for upper-level invited staff. The spirited discussion at one meeting was memorable, and most of it was off the record. One distinguished gentleman proposed a specie he was passionate about—naked mole rats! Oh, how well I remember the gasps that issued from his colleagues and the colorful commentary: How can you compare them to snow leopards or tigers? They are hideous creatures, wrinkled barbarians; there isn't an ounce of cuteness or drama in them, and no one will come see them. But they didn't know the depth of the purse or the persuasive powers of the trustee who thought that naked mole rats had much to teach the public. He believed that unloved, unattractive species are as integral to the health of our environment as their cuddly brethren endowed with sleek fur or those with iridescent feathers. Never underestimate a rich man with a quirky passion project.

What I did not know at the time was that our Curator of Mammals had acquired a group of naked mole rats from South Africa about a year before, and had hoped to exhibit them in the Mouse House. However, their rarity, behavior, and appearance suggested the need for a more prominent venue. I have little doubt that the trustee who promoted this exhibit so strongly had heard about the presence of these strange animals in the collection and decided to become their champion.

◆ ◆ ◆

What is a naked mole rat? Is it one of those mythical, filthy, villainous rodents that inhabit garbage dumps, raid city dumpsters, and terrorize subway riders? Are they afflicted with a nasty skin condition that leads to hair loss? Nothing could be further from the truth. Indeed, naked mole rats are not closely related to either moles or rats. They are more like cute guinea pigs or prickly porcupines than rats, and although they are part of the 2,000-member rodent order, they belong to an altogether different family than the common rat. And like all rodents, they have unique dentition: no canines, only two upper and two lower incisors that grow throughout their lives: gnawing is a rodent specialty.

These critters, barely longer than a man's thumb, are pink, nearly perfectly hairless, and can wield their long incisors like chopsticks or miniature swords. Scientists have discovered that they live in societies ruled by a queen, in cities larger than several football fields, housing some 25-dozen workers who live to protect and serve their queen and her numerous offspring.

Even more surprising than their subterranean lifestyle is the hierarchical structure of their communities, somewhat akin to our lower and upper classes, or bees or termites if you prefer. The queen rules the colony with an iron fist, fighting to maintain her dominance over the lowly workers who do all the grunt work: digging tunnels, searching for food, and caring for her young. Like human societies, naked mole rat colonies include powerful males and soldiers. And, like the lives of many of our estimable trustees, their private lives in the sandy soils of East Africa are fascinating and veiled in secrecy.

♦ ♦ ♦

The rest of the trustees eventually fell in line and agreed, along with the zoo's director and the mammal curator, to get on board with the naked mole rat project. Designs for an ambitious exhibition that would show the secret underground lives of these mysterious creatures were drawn up. The execution of the project, first inspired by the mammal curator, began in the Exhibitions and Graphic Arts Department, appropriately and affectionately known by the acronym EGAD. And, as is necessary with every large-scale project, fundraising began to supplement the generous contribution of the trustee who had championed the exhibit in the first place. But the fundraising staff scratched their heads. Slogans were thought up, then discarded: "Come see the African Queen…and her soldiers," "Bewitching Burrowing Beauties," "Not Just Another Pretty Face." The fundraisers knew this was going to be difficult and quite different from asking donors to pay for a tiger exhibition, but they still had to find a sizeable sum.

After some initial arm-twisting, gifts of varied sizes begun to accrue. EGAD worked feverishly to make the exhibit function within our World of Darkness space. Naked mole rats lead their lives underground and abhor light; this is why they are (nearly) blind. The animal curators conferred on where to acquire more animals, and the vet advised on the quarantine procedures that must be in place for all new arrivals. The nutritionist pondered the best possible diet protocol, a mix of varied root crops. Mole rats are super sensitive to vibrations and noise, so the curator worried about how to isolate them from the hubbub created by throngs of visitors. There was talk of double-glass walls and embedding the exhibit in noise-muffling sand.

Within months the exhibition was nearly ready to make its public debut, but there was one problem. Like any new addition, it needed a name. If you have visited zoos or museums, you've seen that buildings and exhibits often bear the name or names of major donors, like the Leila Acheson Wallace World of Birds, the Carter Giraffe Building, the Aitken Sea Bird Colony, and so on. But having one's name so directly tied to—let's face it… rats—proved problematic.

With only days to the splashy public opening and all the attendant press hoopla, the zoo director hosted the usual trustee preview of the new exhibition. Linen-covered tables laden with expertly catered nibbles and champagne were arranged in the building, which was not yet open to the public. The trustees arrived in their chauffeured limousines, looking like the best of New York's beautiful people: men like penguins in their tuxes, women in ermine stoles, all eager to see how the staff had created an exhibit of animals that would otherwise remain invisible and unappreciated. They walked along the long expanse of glass where cutaways of tunnels in the sand showed the animals digging, eating, lazing around, and performing their tasks of daily living. In amazement, the trustees exclaimed, "Look at those incisors!"

"Their skin is so pink and so sensitive!"

"Where's the queen?"

"I had no idea they had separate bedrooms, nurseries, pantries, and toilets!"

After the initial excitement, the director spoke. "I know how you all enjoy having exhibits or species named after yourselves."

A murmur went through the assembled crowd, and they looked at one another uncomfortably.

The director continued, "So I have decided to name each of these animals after one of you." Audible gasps were heard. The admiration for the critters went only so far.

"But we still haven't met our fundraising target, so we will *remove* your name if you make an additional contribution." The director smiled, and a wave of relieved titters vibrated through the group.

"Was he for real?" one fundraiser asked another, out of earshot. "I have no idea, but he sure gave them a kick in the pants," laughed the other. "I bet we will raise the balance pretty quickly."

The trustees, lovers of beauty and unlikely champions of the homely mole rats, inspired a fascination among the many who came to see this unique exhibit. For months, people were lined up four deep in front of the exhibit. Ever since it opened, scientists the world over have been investigating the naked mole rat's DNA with an eye toward helping humans. It turns out that these animals possess remarkable biological attributes most people covet: unusually long, healthy lives; no bone loss as they age; and vitality in advanced age. Best of all, they seem to defy cancer and have neuro-protective proteins that serve as a barrier against Alzheimer's disease. If they could yield those priceless secrets, might we appreciate them even more? Who knows? With these new discoveries, it may become stylish and sexy to raise funds for ever-grander naked mole rat exhibitions and research.

I walked over to the exhibit after the crowds had dissipated, and watched them sleeping in a pile, thinking that, with a little imagination, they could well be newborn puppies.

CHAPTER 25

The Amazing, Exotic Animal Show

There is a good reason why animal shows on television are perennial favorites: with their fascinating adaptations for survival and often bizarre behaviors, animals have the capacity to amaze us. From *Animal Planet* to *Dog Whisperer*, *Lassie*, or *Crocodile Hunter*, these shows are watched by millions of viewers. Whether scientists discover a heretofore hidden secret about an animal's life, highlight animal phobias, show adorable baby animals, or provide advice on the care of pets, there is always an audience ready to gobble the information. And the weirder, the freakier, the wilder the show, the higher the audience ratings. It seems that we have evolved to have an insatiable appetite for knowledge about the other two million species that share our diverse kingdom: *Animalia*.

After a stressful day at work, who wants to hear about loose nukes, government corruption, or financial collapses? Comfortable slippers, a glass of wine, and a relaxing show about animals is all many folks want. But all of these shows are not created equal. Some are downright silly, some sappy, some overly sensational. Only a few provide a balanced representation of the animal world, and all too few focus on what's really important—wildlife conservation.

Perhaps because of this ever-widening interest in animals, there's a concurrent trend to air programs on animal rights. And for those in the know in the zoo community, "animal rights" has become a code word for anti-zoo. This is exactly what was on my mind when Timmy, one of my supervisors, came to me with what sounded like an attractive proposition at first. He had fielded a call from a television station, and came into my office excited at the prospect of being a featured guest.

We were always chasing free publicity for our education programs, and here a cable station was giving us an opportunity to make a public appearance. Though it was a small local outlet, we relished the idea of speaking directly to viewers to convey the excitement of our programs. And of course, they asked us to bring live animals. That was the real draw.

Normally, I'd have jumped at the chance, but around that time there had been an unusually active period of protests against zoos by animal rights do-gooders. Not that there is anything wrong with wanting animals to be treated with respect and care—this is what we did every day at the zoo—but these groups had an unstated agenda: to close all zoos and "free" the animals. We called them bunny huggers. I was concerned that my staff members would be inadvertently drawn into a discussion that could become difficult if the interviewer had an animal rights agenda. To avoid such a possibility, I asked Timmy to call the station's manager and ask to speak with the program's producer to learn what the format of the program was to be, and what exactly had they hoped to achieve with our appearance.

Timmy, a highly competent member of my staff, said, "Don't worry so much about it. If they throw me a curve ball, I can handle it."

Still, I worried. As Senior Vice President of Education, it was my job to protect the impeccable reputation of our institution. "I know you are good on your feet, Timmy, but please do call."

"OK, boss," he said.

The following day I learned that the producer was rather vague about the program's goal. Aha, I thought, they may want to delve into a discussion that would be unproductive.

"Timmy," I said, "It may not be worth it to travel all the way out to this dinky station and potentially get embroiled in something troublesome. You know that you can't argue with these nuts."

"Boss, I read you loud and clear, but you can trust me. It'll be alright, I can mention the winter zoo camp programs."

Now he had me. He knew that our registration was low and that our advertising budget was zero; this kind of direct appeal to viewers in an affluent area would be very helpful.

"Well, I'll tell you what," I considered, "I'll give you my approval on one condition."

"Sure, what is it?"

"I want you to bring me footage from the show so I can preview it before it's aired."

"No problem, I'll be sure to get it, but please don't worry. It'll be totally fine."

◆ ◆ ◆

Two weeks passed and the date of the show was fast approaching. I was becoming quite anxious about my decision and sorry I had relented. What if Timmy gets trapped into something he can't handle, like the standard moralistic gobbledygook from people who have no clue about the role of our zoos in protecting hundreds of thousands of acres of wildlife habitat around the globe? I was praying that the show would not be aired before I had a chance to see what was taped in the studio.

Two days after a small contingent of keepers accompanied the animals and Timmy to the television station, he came into my office, beaming.

"How did it go?" I asked immediately. "Did they ask you any stupid questions?"

"No, no, it was fine… really."

I noticed the tiny hesitation.

"Did you bring me the footage?" I asked.

"Well… uh… yes, I did," he said.

"You sound like you are dragging your feet, Timmy. Was there a problem?"

"No. You want to see it?"

"Of course."

"OK, meet me in the screening room in a half-hour, I'll set up the projector," he sounded a bit resigned.

I had rarely found a half-hour to last this long. I kept glancing at my watch and couldn't focus on my work until I had seen the footage. Somehow, I had a bad feeling about the whole thing. I went downstairs and sat in front of the screen. Timmy and his assistant, John, were there already.

"Ready?" Timmy asked, and flicked the projector switch.

The show opened with some music and then panned to the interviewer, an attractive young woman sitting comfortably in an easy chair. Timmy sat opposite her. She inquired about the first animal he had brought. Timmy went to the back of the set, where the animals were stored in holding cases and came out smiling, carrying a dove.

The bird sat on his hand and the interviewer began asking fairly innocuous questions, while attempting to reach and touch the bird. The bird flinched and flew up. Timmy looked visibly distressed. He tried to be cool but started running around the set to catch the bird. Every time he almost had it, the bird got away. It flew high up into the rafters above the set. I gasped and uttered a profanity. He paused the film.

"Calm down," Timmy said, "It gets better."

"I can't believe this, Tim, it looks so damn incompetent," I said, and thought I noticed a bit of a smirk on his face. He started coughing.

"Why didn't you bring a more impressive bird?"

He didn't answer and just turned the projector back on.

I couldn't believe my eyes. The bird was nowhere to be seen. Instead, I saw feathers floating down in slow motion from the ceiling, sad remnants of the hapless dove.

"You killed it? You killed the bird! How could you? Our name is mud!" I shouted.

He didn't respond, just went into a kind of choking, coughing fit.

The interviewer attempted to be gentle and said, "Let's go to a commercial break and then I'm sure we'll find the bird and move on to one of Tim's other animals."

I groaned. My stomach was in knots. The next scene showed Tim, now smiling, walking out with a young crocodile in his arms, a bit of tape keeping its powerful jaws closed. Despite its youth, the animal was about five feet in length and the interviewer leaned back when Tim approached her.

"Why is there tape on his mouth?" she asked, her eyes, trained on the long snout.

"Well, we wouldn't want him to have a snack of your finger, would we now?" Timmy joked with her. "Would you like to see how it moves?" he asked.

"Sure, if you don't think he can get away, like the bird," she said.

Timmy placed the animal on the carpet gently. Just as he put it down the tape seemed to get loose and the huge jaws snapped open. The interviewer gasped and jumped up from her seat. The critter swung his head to one side then another, while Tim tried to grab him from behind, keeping his hands away from the impressive teeth. But under the warm lights of the studio lighting system, the reptile became animated and took off. The woman screamed. Timmy got down and, with horror, I saw him crawling on his knees, ineffectually trying to grab the animal. He called to a keeper who had been in the back on standby. Both were now in hot pursuit of the animal, and I was on the verge of a heart attack.

"Shit! Damn! Shit!" The stunning and unexpected display of clumsiness pushed me to the limit, and at that moment my reptilian brain kicked in. I was appalled by the scene unfolding on the screen and the impact it would have on our—my—reputation.

That was when Tim and John simultaneously broke into peals of wild laughter. They sounded like two hyenas.

"Boss, boss, take it easy, it's not real," Tim could hardly choke out the words.

"What?" I said. "What the hell is it then?"

They kept laughing so hard they were sputtering.

"No really, it didn't happen this way. John, turn off the projector," Tim tried to yell over John's convulsive guffaws.

I was more than confused. I felt my cheeks redden with embarrassment.

It took me a while to regain my composure, after which I said sternly, "I want an explanation, Tim."

"Remember how worried you were about my performance?" he said.

"Well…" I hesitated.

It was true, I had been, perhaps a tiny bit more than the situation warranted.

"So, this is what? My punishment?"

They laughed in unison. I saw how amused they were.

"So how did you get this, this, dare I call it… show footage?"

"We set up the classroom like a studio set and shot it yesterday after work."

"But the plants and all! It looked so authentic," I said.

"We are *not* amateurs," Tim said with pride.

"But who was the interviewer?" I asked still incredulous at how they managed to pull off such a stunt.

"Oh, that's John's new girlfriend. She's studying acting."

I began to laugh. Soon I was doubled over, wiping tears from my eyes. It was quite a clever prank.

"Maybe you missed your calling, Tim," I said. "Ever thought about television production?"

He didn't reply at first, then threw his second bomb.

"By the way, see this other camera, on the side of the counter?" he asked me.

"Yes, what about it?"

"We filmed your reactions to our amazing, exotic animal show."

Suddenly I felt like one of the animals whose elusive secrets have been filmed by Sir David Attenborough.

"You got me, Tim. I've got to hand it to you and, yes, I'll try to be more relaxed… next time."

CHAPTER 26

Rachel's Secret

It wasn't just that the millennium was about to descend, but 1999 would be a big year in my personal and work life: our daughter would be married, my father would celebrate his 90th birthday, we'd move to a new house, and at the Bronx Zoo the Congo Gorilla Forest would finally open to the public with great fanfare.

A decade in the planning, the groundbreaking two-story gorilla exhibit would cause a collective gasp among zoo professionals across the world. With its uncanny reproduction of the western lowland gorilla's habitat deep in the rainforests of the Congo, the exhibition opened a window on the lives of the most interesting human relative. Now city dwellers removed from the mystery of remote jungles could experience the magic of seeing gorillas going about their daily lives, foraging and playing as they do in nature.

A floor-to-ceiling glass partition would be the only separation between human parents with boys and girls in tow and gorilla families: mothers cradling infants, aunts grooming older youngsters, juvenile males swinging from vines, and an imposing male silverback keeping a watchful eye on his troop. In all, two troops of gorillas would make their home in this six-and-a-half acre slice of the Bronx.

As soon as it opened, the gorilla forest boggled the minds of visitors, journalists, critics, and zoo peers. How did we manage the illusion of a lush, shaded, humid rainforest trail reverberating with the calls of hornbills and hoopoes, the whooshing of waterfalls, and splashes of butterfly color flitting among the giant trees? This, in a place where outside the gates police cars cruised blighted neighborhoods, ambulance sirens pierced the air, and double-length city buses spewed exhaust.

It was the ingenuity of our designers, curators, educators, and visionary director William G. Conway who recreated the Congo forest indoors, along a third-of-a-mile adventure trail. Here awestruck visitors meandered through treetop lookouts, vibrant meadows, and the cathedral-like rainforest, whose trees can reach somewhere between 100-150 feet in the wild. At 43 million dollars, the most expensive city exhibit ever, Congo Gorilla Forest was home to some 400 species of plants and more than four-dozen species of animals, from monkeys to okapis, red river hogs, monitor lizards, and pythons, among others. But to me that experiential feast was not the most amazing feature of this grand exhibition. It was a secret space accessible only to very special visitors.

It took a decade of planning and fundraising to build this exhibition. Through all those years, I attended dozens of meetings with designers, architects, and curators. We all had the same goal: to immerse the visitors in the experience so fully that they'd come away caring about gorillas and their habitat, enough to participate in the efforts to save them from extinction. The difficulties ranged from the physical to the conceptual. Recreating a complex ecosystem indoors was a huge challenge: fabricating nearly ten miles of artificial vines, designing a dozen waterfalls, and sculpting 45,000 square feet of space. Inventing new ways to make visitors truly pay attention and take responsibility for the survival of gorillas was quite a different challenge. To that the end, we gave visitors the ability to vote on which conservation project they wished to support with their admission fee.

There was one difference between me and the other planners: I focused my attention not only on the masses of the public who'd come, but on the children and teachers who would participate in our special programs. I felt that with them we'd have a deeper opportunity to create budding conservationists. Putting our brains together, we conspired to build a classroom unlike any other in the world: a beautiful space, high in the treetops, decorated with African artwork and artifacts. But that wasn't all. Here, in the middle of the space, we would open what looked like an elegantly paneled closet door to reveal a small group of gorillas sitting just behind glass, right there, in the classroom with the students. With no other visitors to make noise or jostle for a better viewing spot, the kids in *this* classroom would have the gorillas to themselves.

◆◆◆

In early June 1999, the zoo was in a last-minute flurry of activity preparing for the grand opening. Everyone had the usual preopening jitters, but I couldn't wait for the reaction to the gorillas in our secret classroom space. I wanted to test it out on just one child. And then it struck me: in just a few days my ten-year-old niece Rachel would be visiting from Berlin, Germany. A sophisticated child, Rachel had traveled extensively around the world and seen more amazing sights than most of her peers and probably many adults. I reasoned that if my secret gorillas captivated Rachel, they'd impress every other child who came for classes. I couldn't wait to get her to the zoo before the public opening. Rachel lived in a city that had a very old tradition of animal exhibition. The Berlin Zoo opened in 1844, more than half a century before the Bronx Zoo, but by the late nineties it had fallen behind in modern exhibition techniques. I knew Rachel had visited there, and I wanted to best that experience for my young visitor who loved having an aunt who worked at the zoo.

A week before the public opening, Rachel and I walked through the exhibit. We saw keepers polishing the glass, moving food pans, and rearranging anything that might disturb the illusion. Rachel stood before one exhibit and whispered, "I haven't been to Africa yet, but now I don't have to go."

"Why are you whispering, Rachel?" I asked.

"This is amazing. Look at the mandrill. His face looks painted," she whispered back.

"Wait. You ain't seen nothin' yet," I told her.

I could barely drag her away from the public space, but I itched to move onto the second level where the classroom was located. Eventually I succeeded in tearing her away from observing the red river hogs.

We entered the silent classroom.

"Wow," she said, "I can see the exhibit from here." She came close to the glass wall, behind which two hornbills sat in the treetops.

"Who will come here?"

"Kids like you," I said.

She looked around the room, asking me questions about the exquisite geometric patterns of the Kente cloth decorations and the various masks in the room. I was happy to explain that the cloth and masks were not only beautiful, but represented the history and culture of various African peoples.

When I felt she was ready for something new I said, "Rachel, do you want to see the secret of this room?"

She looked at me, puzzled.

"Now, promise you'll remain very quiet," I said.

She nodded.

I opened the "closet" door and right against the glass sat Julia, the nineteen-year-old gorilla, snacking on some leaves. Rachel gasped and approached. She was stunned into complete silence. I stood aside, watching her watch Julia.

Julia's eyes had an intensity and real focus. It was clear she wasn't simply staring out for lack of a better thing to do. She was assessing Rachel. And as I stood there I began reflecting not only on what Rachel thought, but Julia as well. Julia's intelligent eyes made me a bit uncomfortable.

Then I remembered what I had read about human zoos that had become popular in the late 1800s, when Carl Hagenbeck, an animal dealer from Hamburg, Germany, began exhibiting indigenous people from Samoa, Sudan, and the Arctic regions. His human exhibitions traveled to "civilized" cities like London, Paris, and Berlin where they were greeted by throngs of jeering visitors. I made an effort to push these thoughts away: at least here, in this exhibition, we did everything humanly possible to engender respect for these intelligent primates, to have visitors understand them as ambassadors from the wild.

Julia shifted slightly, turned and looked directly at Rachel. Maybe it was Rachel's diminutive size or her gentle blue eyes, but Julia seemed to reciprocate the girl's fascination. Julia's open round face was inches from Rachel's. She seemed to have a playful smile on her wise-looking face. Rachel lifted her palm and placed it on the glass. A moment later Julia put her large hand on the other side of the glass, as if to touch Rachel's. These two were communicating on a level that defied words.

Rachel turned toward me and whispered, "She likes me."

I had a hard time separating the newly-acquainted friends, but it was getting late.

"Rachel, we have to go now and we need to give Julia some privacy," I said.

"Does she live here alone, in this classroom," Rachel inquired as we headed toward the parking lot.

"No. She lives with her troop in the exhibit area below the classroom, but this secret place is off the exhibit, a place the gorillas can come to when they feel like having some privacy."

"Like my room," Rachel said with a smile, then added, "I will never forget her and I'll keep this a secret."

That was exactly what I'd hoped she'd say.

It turned out that the exhibition and its stars, the gorillas, made the huge impact we hoped for. In the first ten years, the visitors to this exhibition alone contributed nearly eleven million dollars to the conservation of gorillas in Africa. And I never tired of seeing the faces of the students and teachers who came to our special classroom and discovered Rachel's secret.

CHAPTER 27

Namesakes

Outside of Hollywood, the Big Apple attracts more celebrities than anywhere else in the country. Here in swanky Manhattan hotels and performance venues, actors, sports figures, musicians, and politicians mingle with peers, regale journalists, and chit-chat with gossip columnists. And posing for cameras is nearly always a part of the ritual of seeing and being seen. Sometimes they even—gasp—venture to the outer boroughs and come to places like the Bronx Zoo that may seem to be on an entirely different continent.

Indeed, over the more than one hundred years of the zoo's esteemed history it has become rather *de rigueur* to pay a visit and meet its celebrity animals: one celebrity to another! One such animal was Nachman the wallaby.

Thinking about a wallaby might bring up Kanga and Roo, or maybe Captain Kangaroo, but hardly a soul would link this small feisty marsupial with the 42nd president of the United

States. The Bronx Zoo's photo files would show that a senior staff member of the Education Division introduced President Clinton and his brother Roger to Nachman the wallaby in the early 2000s. That is a fact on record, but one might wonder how *this* wallaby came to acquire a Yiddish name and serve as the zoo's goodwill ambassador.

◆◆◆

Shortly after my father's funeral, I received a most unusual call. Kathleen, the young woman who cared for the collection of Children's Zoo animals, was on the line, telling me somewhat haltingly, "I just received a baby wallaby. Its mother has rejected it. He is so tiny and beautiful! I'd like to name him Nachman, after your father. If it's okay with you, that is."

"A wa-lla-by?" I said slowly, "Is that what you said, Kathleen?"

"Yes."

I was still grieving and not inclined to smile at anything, but a wide grin grew on my face. I knew my father would have gotten a kick out of this unusual tribute. This would be the only wallaby in the world with a Yiddish name.

I chuckled and said, "Yes, of course, go ahead, Kathleen, and take good care of him," all the while wondering if my father's friends would see this as a disrespectful tribute. *Naming a wild animal after your dear departed father, may he rest in peace? What were you thinking?*

Kathleen was delighted and reminded me of how my father played her favorite songs whenever she visited our home. He knew a vast repertoire of songs by heart: Yiddish,

Polish, Russian, Italian, and nearly the entire Beatles collection. He'd taught himself how to play the keyboard when he was in his late seventies and his remarkable ear enabled him to play and sing on-key in his rich baritone.

What surprised me most about Kathleen's tribute was that she didn't know that, indirectly, my father had been responsible for acquiring the wallabies for the Children's Zoo exhibition in the first place. My work colleagues always enjoyed my father's charming personality and he was invited to many zoo events.

When I took him through the Children's Zoo to show him some improvements we had made, he asked me, "Why don't you have any kangaroos here? Kids love them."

I explained that our space wasn't adequate for kangaroos but he persisted, "Aren't there some smaller kangaroo species?"

He was far from an animal expert, but he watched all the animal specials on television. He got me thinking. After discussions with our animal experts, it was decided that we could include wallabies in the future. And so, in time, a wallaby exhibit became a popular Children's Zoo attraction. I smiled, remembering all that as I hung up the phone after Kathleen made her request to name the little orphan after my father.

◆◆◆

One of the most urgent concerns was to provide little pinky Nachman with a substitute for Mama wallaby's milk. In nature joeys have the remarkable instinct of navigating from the birth canal to the mother's teat in her pouch when they are no longer than one inch! There they attach themselves to the teat for continuous nourishment; but Nachman's fate would be different. He would become completely dependent on Kathleen, his human mother.

The interesting thing about wallaby milk is that its composition changes dramatically as the joey grows. In the earliest stages, it is laden with carbohydrates; later on, fats predominate. (Human milk also changes composition, but the changes are small compared with marsupials.) Nachman's survival odds were long and the challenges enormous: to find a facsimile of wallaby milk, obtain the correct variant as time went on, find a reliable supplier, and stay up nights for eye-dropper feedings.

Lucky for Nachman, Kathleen found a source for early-, mid-, and late-lactation wallaby milk replacements called Wombaroo and Biolac. By the time Nachman weighed about two pounds, he grew a silky coat of gray hair and no longer resembled his former puny half-pound hairless self. He was sweet and feisty but still needed to spend most of his time in the specially-designed pouch that Kathleen wore slung over her shoulder, to hold him on her belly, like any good wallaby mama. The bonding was an important aspect of little Nachman's well-being. He and Kathleen became inseparable.

When he was old enough to hop out of the pouch on a regular basis and cavort with Kathleen's pet dogs, he lived in her apartment on zoo grounds. Nothing but the finest accommodations would suffice for this pampered marsupial. Nachman had his own room with a television set he enjoyed watching animal shows on. In the morning, he'd clamber into his pouch even when he was way too big to be carried, like toddlers who still like to ride in the stroller when they can navigate perfectly well on their own. And his birthday parties with cake and banners were no less elaborate. When the furry Nachman was old enough to make a public debut, he got his own employee photo nametag, and Kathleen chauffeured him around in a silk-lined pouch while she traversed the zoo on her electric cart. The sight of Nachman craning his neck out of the pouch to see the world as they drove by caused even employees to chuckle, and they were accustomed to strange animal shenanigans.

Nachman mesmerized the visitors. They couldn't get enough stories about this orphan's special care. Like his namesake, he charmed everyone with his approachable persona and lively blue eyes. With his employee ID tag, Nachman behaved like a well-paid top-notch PR man. If it hadn't been for Kathleen's dedication and know-how, he would surely not have survived, and survival was something the wallaby had in common with his namesake: Nachman the man was a Holocaust survivor.

In no time, it became a Bronx Zoo tradition for every V.I.P. who came to the zoo to visit and be photographed with Nachman. Major celebrities ventured out from Manhattan to see the world-famous Bronx Zoo exhibitions and say hello to the furry creature whose very survival summed up the level of care devoted to all the zoo's wild animals. From President Bill Clinton to numerous stars of screen and television, musicians such as Sheryl Crowe, and sports figures like Lance Armstrong in his heyday took time out of their visit to have their photo taken with Nachman.

Kathleen would take them behind the scenes and begin her introduction saying, "Now that you have come to see this wonderful creature, I must first tell you how he acquired his name." The audience would look a bit baffled and eager to touch the wallaby's incredibly soft fur, but Kathleen continued, "Once I met a man who inspired me with his artwork and his music. He taught himself how to play and paint when he was well into his old age. His name was Nachman, and he made me believe that anything is possible if you put your mind to it... even raising a wallaby."

CHAPTER 28

Double Takes

We humans seem to know what *real* means, at least most of the time. The tree in our yard, the dog chewing on our slippers, the hot coffee cup in our hand, we recognize all these objects as real. Even things we can't see are real to us, like the love we feel for our children, husbands, or wives, and issues like hunger and fiscal recessions.

There are times, however, when our sense of what's real is tested. Tangible things like counterfeit money, well-made faux pearls, or a product that seemed fine at the time of purchase but fell apart almost immediately—all of these can fool us. Intangible things can confuse us even more, like a bargain that seems too good to be true, or a job agreement that does not materialize. We can even be fooled by things we were sure were real, like a love that has evaporated, or a smile we mistook for a sneer. Our large brains allow us to feel chagrined when we realize we've been fooled; but I wondered, do animals ever have such difficulties? Do they ever confuse the real for the unreal and vice versa?

When we bought a house in the country, we had an encounter with the wildlife there that made me wonder. We had brought as many decorative items from the city as seemed appropriate for our house surrounded by woods: wind chimes, flower pots, and outdoor sculptures. Since we were auction aficionados in the city, we snagged wonderful cast iron pieces: hitching posts with elegant horse heads, a chubby goose, and two ornately antlered deer of indeterminate species. We placed them strategically to enhance our garden.

We always enjoyed looking out at the serene vista outside our windows. Often, we were rewarded by the flash of the red crest of a pileated woodpecker, blue jays noisily pushing away competitors from the feeder, or the shadow of a red fox in hot pursuit of its prey. On snowy days, there were always footprints left behind by deer, raccoons, even the occasional coyote. The mammals were generally elusive, but one day we saw a sight we'll always remember.

It was an early December morning. Snow had fallen overnight and white bonnets covered the bushes outside. I had just made a pot of coffee and was walking toward the counter to pour it, when a shadow in the corner of my eye caught my attention as I passed the window. A large buck emerged from a thicket of mountain laurel on the hill behind our deck. Majestic in his demeanor, he ambled down, trampling the small azalea bushes we'd planted. He was so impressive, I couldn't be annoyed. He made his way toward our circular driveway, anchored by an ornamental cherry tree.

We had placed our deer sculptures right below that tree to welcome arriving visitors. The buck approached cautiously and stood near them. What was he thinking? A few moments later, a female deer made her appearance, fashionably late. I knew it was breeding season and wistfully imagined this was their designated love spot, but nothing of the kind happened. Now, they both stood spellbound by what could have been kindred spirits, though these seemed frozen.

Both my husband and I stood glued to the window waiting to see how this encounter would unfold. For what seemed a long while, both the flesh-and-blood deer and those wrought in iron stood motionless, the former contemplating their inert species mates. Normally deer are super vigilant, but they seemed so entranced by the sight that nothing could distract them. The grayish brown winter coat of the visitors looked eerily similar to the patina of the metal figures.

Gradually both the buck and the female approached the sculptures. They stood face to face and for an infinitesimal moment it looked as if they were making a decision. Finally, action: they began sniffing the sculptures, first front, then back. They circled them cautiously, lest the cold metal simulacra be resurrected from their torpor and challenge the intruders. Another round of sniffing. The deer's sense of smell is infinitely keener than a human's. I thought they'd smell the metal and immediately recognize it as an alien substance, but it didn't seem that way.

After the sniffing ceremony, they stood there still, as if contemplating the meaning of reality. The episode reminded me of my own unreal experiences watching the giraffe munching on a bird, or snapping photos of crocodiles while a lioness was getting ready to make me a meal. I would have loved to know what conclusion the deer had drawn from the strange encounter, and if I hadn't been so mesmerized myself, I'd have documented the meeting with my camera. Of course, no documentation would ultimately solve the mystery. Physicists have observed that reality contains mysteries of its own and that simply observing it can influence its behavior.

In the end, the buck pawed and scraped the ground, most likely leaving the scent emanating from the glands between his hooves, just in case the metal impostors came to life. He wanted to be sure they don't get a sudden urge to follow the doe.

♦ ♦ ♦

On a different occasion, I discovered that humans can be as mistaken about reality as these deer were. It was another fall and our son, daughter-in-law, and granddaughters had come for the weekend to admire the magnificent seasonal leaf display. By then it was dusk and we were just about ready to sit down to dinner when the girls spotted a large female white-tailed deer emerging from the shrubs on the hill behind our house, the very hill the deer who had encountered our sculpted deer had come from.

"Mommy, look at the deer, fast before it runs away!" one of the girls called out excitedly.

My daughter-in-law, the girls, and I pressed our noses to the French door facing the hill. The animal stood there, nearly motionless.

"Is it a boy or a girl?" the younger granddaughter asked.

"It is a girl," I said. "Actually, she's a grown-up, like a lady."

"But how can you tell lady deer from men deer?"

I expected this question.

"This time of year, a male would have antlers."

My little lesson was soon over because the female pranced away and the girls lost interest. I called my son, who had been working on a project in the basement, to come up for dinner.

He came up excited.

"Did you all see that buck with that rack of antlers?" he asked.

"What buck?" I was mystified.

"The one on the hill, the one I heard you talking about."

I looked at him and wondered if he was hallucinating.

"Daddy, we saw a lady deer," the girls chimed in.

"But I saw a rack of antlers this big," Jeremy spread his arms nearly four feet.

That was when the fragility of reality hit me squarely in the nose.

"I guess sometimes we can't be sure of what we have seen," I said.

"Yeah, never trust an eyewitness," my husband said, coming up the stairs from the basement.

I looked out again and it struck me that from his angle of view, my son could have mistaken the dry branches hanging over the area where the deer had stood as a rack of antlers.

CHAPTER 29

Life's Not a Bowl of Cherries

It was a glorious summer day in the Berkshires. Woken early by our hard-working woodpeckers, I put up a pot of coffee, then settled on the deck to watch the ruby-throated hummingbirds flitting around the red geranium pots. Like emerald-encrusted Cartier miniatures come to life, they made me pause between sips—trying to freeze the motion of their 50-beats-per-second wings— impossible! My coffee went cold. I looked around our yard, pleased that David had planted the geraniums on Mother's Day. They were better than feeders for attracting the hummers.

That morning we decided to drive into Great Barrington to pick up some groceries, and I had seen that there was a special on Bing cherries, my favorite summer fruit. Maybe it was the sight of the hummers hovering over each geranium that whetted my appetite for this sensuous fruit. We entered the Price Chopper and each of us took a different aisle so we could finish shopping quickly and get back to enjoying our garden with its birds, butterflies, and lush flowerbeds.

I headed straight toward the counter laden with luscious-looking cherries. An instant later, my body flew sideways as my foot caught under a rolled-up rubber matting. I screamed—at least I think I did, because everything went fuzzy. The pain was unbearable. I struggled uselessly to get up, but my body was limp and clammy. Then I saw a circle of faces above me, and David reaching for my hand. "You'll be OK, honey. Hold on a moment, the ambulance is on its way."

As it turned out, I wasn't the only one with a yen for cherries. It seems others had come, sampling the irresistible fruit and spitting the pits onto the floor. When I headed toward the counter, I had stepped on some pits and rolled on them as if they were ball bearings. The one surgeon in the area was unavailable that weekend because she had suffered an appendicitis attack. So, several local hospital nurses shot me full of morphine and maneuvered me into our new Subaru wagon with its front seat down, making an impromptu gurney, and told David to drive me to a hospital in Manhattan.

I will never quite understand how David managed to make the three-hour journey safely, with me alternately crying and moaning the entire time. It turned out that I had shattered my ankle, breaking all three bones in it and tearing all the ligaments and tendons. David informed me later that the sight of my foot hanging by a thread had scared him witless. Two surgeries later, with my foot held together by metal plates and screws, I was able to leave the hospital in a wheelchair. The chief of physical therapy informed me, "I doubt you'll ever walk again. With a lot of therapy, you might be able to get around on crutches, but that'll be months from now." The pain and his grim pronouncement made me furious. I'll show him, I thought.

David arranged for a ramp to be built so he could wheel me up the deck of our Berkshire home and directly into the living room. We lucked out, having a ground floor bedroom and bath. Returning to work would be impossible for a long while. Our home in New Rochelle seemed to be an endless maze constructed of nothing but stairs, stairs, stairs. And access to my office at the zoo, likewise, involved stairs. Handicapped accessibility became as real to me as the constant pain and the struggle to avoid the pills that made me groggy.

I decided that the best way to keep the pain at bay would be to plunge immediately back into work. I worked out a plan to have daily conference calls with my staff. The secretary would send me FedEx envelopes with curriculum materials to review, new program approvals, project management schedules, budgets, and performance reviews. The local FedEx delivery driver, unaccustomed to such regular deliveries in a farming community, seemed stunned. Maybe he thought something strange was going on. It wasn't until I explained where I worked that he took delight in bringing me my daily dose of zoo, and even told me that a mama black bear and her cub lived up on the ridge above our house. "I seen 'er a few times on my rounds in these parts," he reported.

But the accident had a silver lining. It was the first time I could remain in the country for a sustained period of time and have the luxury of doing my work sitting in the wheelchair on my deck, pausing to observe the hummingbirds and the masses of Monarchs on the butterfly bushes. There was something so delicious and unexpected about being able to work at a leisurely pace in my pajamas, and communing with nature in a deeper way than I could in my rush-rush Bronx work world. No meetings, no constant phone ringing, no schoolchildren yelling outside my office building, just the sound of bees buzzing around the purple heads of the coneflowers, the woodpeckers whacking the dead trees for insects, and relatives of my old friend Bully making their throaty scraping sounds from across the swamp on the other side of the road.

Soon fall made its appearance, with masses of multicolored leaf piles. How I wished I could walk through them, crunching them under my feet as I had done when I was a girl! We lit the fireplace and sat sipping sherry, listening to the wind. The silence was calming. I could get used to this, I thought. By then David had retired and noticing the new calmer me he asked, "Wouldn't you like this pace all the time?"

"What do you mean?" I sat up, alarmed.

"Well… retirement?"

"You must be kidding, David. You know I'll never retire."

But his question planted the seed of an idea in my mind. It would take more than a year to germinate.

Winter in the Berkshires turned out to be as beautiful as the summer and fall. Puffy blankets of blinding snow covered the shrubs. The occasional white-crowned sparrows perched on the trees looked like unexpected ornaments. Tracks of deer and foxes reminded us daily that life was still out there. Aside from continuing to work daily—even having a staff meeting once, when a group of my supervisors travelled all the way to Massachusetts—I devoted a lot of time to physical therapy. By golly, I was going to beat this wheelchair if it killed me.

Seven months after my accident, David drove me to New York so I could attend a City Council hearing. I had been invited to speak about the dreary state of science education by the chair of the Education Committee. It was exciting to be back into the swing of things, so to speak. I still needed to be maneuvered into the City Hall building via back entrances reserved for wheelchairs. After the hearing, I remained in New York so I could attend a workshop my division had organized for scholars and educators from zoos around the U.S. and abroad. I could not yet return to our super-vertical home, so we stayed in a Marriot hotel. I felt a jolt of energy as I returned to the zoo. Sitting in the Congo Gorilla forest classroom, listening to the presentations, I felt a warm sense of accomplishment. Finally, we were influencing other educators and decision-makers to incorporate ecology as an essential part of education, making it as important as mathematics or social studies.

By the spring, after ten months in a wheelchair, I was finally able to take my first tentative steps on crutches. David had to drive me to work daily and pick me up. It was a chore he was glad to do, as he had been my nurse and helper through-out the entire ordeal. Moving around the zoo on crutches was difficult and my wonderful secretary, Mary, drove me in my electric cart to meetings on the 265-acre campus.

When summer came, I invited my son Jeremy to bring his three-year-old daughter Camille—my first red-headed granddaughter—to the zoo. I took her to the Children's Zoo and delighted in her squeals as she curled up in the heron's nest and climbed the saguaro cactus to see the owl inside. En route there, we passed the old Lion House where Carlos the puma had been housed all those years ago. The building had been closed for years, because it had become outdated. There were plans to turn it into an exhibition on Madagascar one day, but that kind of radical renovation would take years of fundraising. Sixty-two million dollars and two years later it would open to the public. The Reptile House, the zoo's second-oldest exhibit (built in 1900), which the king cobra had escaped from years before, still hung on. The king cobra was bested in 2011 by the escape of a poisonous Egyptian cobra, which was also eventually found inside the building. Despite this, the Reptile House's popularity with visitors never died down. Some things will never change, I thought, as Camille tugged on my arm, pointing to the squirrels.

There was talk about closing the Monkey House with my uncommon marmosets, too, because it also sent the wrong message. After 114 years of operation, it would be closed in 2012. Even the World of Darkness, revolutionary in its time for flipping day and night, so nocturnal creatures like bats could be seen by visitors, was approaching the end of its useful lifespan. It was finally shuttered in 2009 after 40 years of operation. I knew things would continue to change in the future, but each big change needed years of discussion, and there was always more to do. The World of Birds, which had been brand new and startling when I began in 1972, was now showing its age. The birds still flew free in open-fronted exhibits with lovely backgrounds painted by skilled muralists, but even here the smallish exhibits had a museum-y feel. Compared to the expansive Congo Gorilla Forest, they looked dated.

When Camille was done with all the Children's Zoo exhibits, we made the mandatory stop in the petting area. She squealed with delight as she fed handfuls of pellets to the goats. Her squeals reminded me of Claude in his camel barn refuge, and I smiled.

Not only were there exhibition changes in the wind, the administration too had changed. The focus was increasingly on our worldwide conservation and research activities, with a corresponding decrease of funds for the animal facilities. The tug of war over financial support by the different divisions had sharpened. The veterinarians wanted more funds for research on zoonotic diseases; conservationists wanted more for field operations; the exhibition and graphic arts department wanted new exhibits and interpretive panels; and, of course, I wanted more funds for our education activities in the metropolitan area, the rest of the U.S., and overseas. It was hard to see which department would prevail, but international conservation began to look like the big winner. The competition was wearing. It was like fighting insurance companies: endless calls to express your views that get you nowhere.

I had had great success in fundraising for my programs over the years, from federal government, city, state, and private foundations, but the constant chase for dollars to nurture ongoing programs was hard. Everyone wanted to pour money into new programs, but what about support for the ones that had been proven to work?

I returned to my office after the Children's Zoo visit with Camille. She ran straight to my much-too-large for her office chair and climbed in. Too short to reach the desk, she perched on her knees and I watched her from the door. "Bubbi, do you have any crayons for me?' she asked, looking ready to work.

"Open my desk drawer and see," I said.

She pulled out the drawer and dipped her short arm in, all the way up to her shoulder, trying to reach into its depths. She dragged out something black and held it up. "What's this, Bubbi?"

I could hardly believe it. Dried up and a bit shriveled, it was the black glove Rob had given me my first month at the zoo to save my arm from raptor claws. I hadn't realized it had been stuck in there for over thirty years! My trophy.

"Camille, it's a special glove. One day I will tell you a story about it."

Camille found the crayons and began working furiously on a masterpiece. Her arm spun around the paper making brown swirls. She held up her scribbles, "Look, I drew a bear," she chirped, and stared at it proudly. She looked like a miniature zoo curator, I thought, tickled.

There will be new women getting into my chair one of these days, I thought. Maybe soon. One of my major projects, obtaining state accreditation for our master's level teacher course, was close to completion (after a lot of red tape). Maybe it was almost time to turn over the reins to a new generation.

CHAPTER 30

Bandits of Westchester

When I was away in Kenya, my husband had surprised me by building a huge freestanding mahogany deck in the back of our house. He drew up the plans himself, dug the holes in the earth for the supports, and hand-mixed the concrete footings. When I returned, I was delighted and my friends were incredulous. "He did that and took care of the kids? Do you hire him out?" they asked. Their comments reminded me that I could not have succeeded in my demanding job without his help and moral support. As far as I was concerned, David could do everything.

I was so happy with the deck that I planned our daughter's sweet sixteen party on it, and more than three dozen dancing teens could not shake its foundations. We were so tired after the party that we left the chairs and tables out and, exhausted, fell into bed.

Somewhere in the middle of the night, we heard noises out back and Tess the Airedale barked frantically. We lived in one of the safest suburban communities in Westchester county, so I wasn't too alarmed as I shook David awake. But as we made our way down the staircase, the loud noises and Tess's unrelenting growling made us apprehensive. "Sounds as if someone is moving the furniture on the deck," I said, rubbing the sleep out of my eyes.

"Who'd want to steal some plastic chairs?" David said, unconcerned. "But let's see who's making this racket."

We turned on the kitchen light and looked out the window that faced the deck. Like masked bandits, a troop of six oversized raccoons had taken over. Some of them were a bit smaller and might have been kits with a sow, but they were surely well fed! They looked to be a good 25 pounds each. Some stood on the chairs on their hind legs, waving their foot-long ringed tails, trying to peer through the window, their masked faces staring at us, black noses pressed to the glass. Others hissed, barked and yowled, pushing the chairs as if they wanted to load them on a truck. A few chomped on the party goodies we had carelessly failed to pick up.

At first, we thought the kitchen light and deck flood lights would frighten them and they'd run away, but we were dead wrong. It seemed as if our presence encouraged them to show their command of our porch. They ran about as if they were having their own party. We began tapping on the window to frighten them, but they may as well have been laughing, "Who are you to intrude on our fun?"

"David, we have got to get rid of them," I said. "Any ideas?"

"I thought you liked wildlife," he quipped.

"Come on, I'm tired. And need I bring up our squirrel fiasco?" I said. Tess stood near me, trying to stand on her hind legs to see the gray, carnivorous troop on the deck.

"I'm not going out there with so many; maybe if there was one…" David said.

"No, you better not. They can carry canine distemper or rabies, though they sure don't look sick," I said. "Look at them, as fat as the Children's Zoo animals."

"Well, they have it made around here. Plenty of aquatic critters in Manor Park, even in Flint Park: frogs, crustaceans, trees, standing and fallen; lots of goodies in the garbage cans too," David remarked.

"Did you secure our garbage cans?" I remembered suddenly.

"Sure. It wasn't our garbage that attracted them. It was my lovely deck," he smiled.

I tried to recall what I had read about getting rid of nuisance local wildlife. Ammonia soaked rags? Mothballs? Spraying vinegar-laced water at them? None of the ideas made sense, not at night, and not with so many animals. Tess had quieted, seeing that our initial outburst of concern had subsided.

"You know what," David said, "let's go to sleep. Let's leave them alone. I'm sure they won't be here in the morning,"

"OK," I said, too tired to argue and disappointed that David, my can-do-everything man, was no match for these intruders.

He banged on the windows a few more times in a wan effort, but the raccoons ignored him and continued to party undeterred. I went to sleep, trying to block out the noise by pulling the down blanket over my ears. "Maybe we need to import a few coyotes," I mumbled.

What I did not know was that David had already had an encounter with an angry raccoon and was not about to face a whole pack of them. It happened when he was building the sunroom and opened the roof to install insulation and cut openings for the skylights. A raccoon snuck in to snuggle in the insulation in the daytime, and David caught him sauntering out at dusk. No use alarming Annette, he thought and promptly closed up the opening. The raccoon returned from his nocturnal sojourn the next morning and David watched him scrambling up the brick wall to his cozy den. When he found it shut, he put on a spectacular display of ire: scratching with his long claws, growling, hissing, and uttering short plaintive barks. When I heard this, I understood why my Renaissance man was not about to tangle with six raccoon brethren. In fact, one of them may have been the very one denied entrance before.

When we woke up in the morning the raccoons were gone. The only reminder of their invasion were the chairs scattered at odd angles, some turned over, others listing on the deck railing.

♦ ♦ ♦

Several years passed happily without any raccoon encounters, but we were not home free. In the summer of 2004, after breaking my ankle so badly, we stayed for many months at our home in the Berkshires, which luckily had a ground floor bedroom.

In between the daily Fedex packages from work that kept my mind off the pain, David and I had the luxury of time to think for the first time in years. We made a decision: our house in New Rochelle, where we had moved from Larchmont, was now not only unsuitable for us, it was too big and had to be sold. With some trepidation and regret, we called a real estate broker and put the house up for sale. I knew I'd miss our gardens, the orchard, and magnificent rhododendrons, but it was wasteful for two people to live in a fourteen-room house. We'd move to a small New York City apartment and take advantage of the Big Apple's charms in due course, when I retired.

Summer turned to fall, and for the first time I could watch the entire progression of the leaves turning yellow, then red and drifting down in a slow dance, landing in heaps at the front and back of our cottage. One day late in the evening the phone rang, sharp and insistent. Unused to disturbances in our quiet country life, we answered it to find our real estate broker on the line.

"I hate to tell you this, but I have a buyer who wants to see not only your house, but your two-story detached garage."

"Why is that a problem?" I asked.

"Well, I don't know how to say this politely," she hesitated.

"Go on," I encouraged.

"OK, there is a terrible stench coming from the garage. It smells like a dead body," she finally blurted out.

We hadn't been at the house for nearly four months, since there was no way for me to get up the five front steps or the flight of stairs to our bedroom. What had happened? We were mortified.

"Should I call the police?" she asked.

"No, no, perhaps first you can hire someone to open the garage and check out the situation," I said.

My mind raced. Could someone have stashed a murder victim in there? At night, ours was a dark, quiet lane. It might have been possible for someone to hide a dastardly deed, unnoticed by neighbors.

Suddenly David blurted out, "Remember, Annette, I fixed that hole in the garage door before we moved to the cottage?"

"What does that have to do with anything?"

"What if an animal got in and became trapped?"

"Ugh," I said, and my stomach tightened.

◆◆◆

The following week, the real estate agent called again.

"You would not believe the scene of destruction we faced when the garage was opened," she said. I braced myself for her description.

"A couple of raccoons somehow managed to get in, but could not figure out how to get out. They must have tried like hell to escape, because they tore up almost everything you had stored there."

Oh, my God, it was then I remembered: dozens of my father's priceless paintings and my winter clothes had been stored on the second level of the garage! All I could think about was the damage the beasts may had done to my father's life's work.

The agent understood my concern and commiserated.

"I've had those darn bandits in my home too. But don't worry, I have hired a cleaning service to tidy up the mess and get rid of the smell."

"But… but… what about the paintings?"

"I'm sorry. That I can't tell you. You'll have to come when you are better and assess their condition for yourself," she said.

I was horrified. All I could imagine were strips of torn canvas with bits of shredded images my dad had worked so hard to create. Those damn raccoons! I was furious at the situation and yet also sorry for the poor critters. They were just looking for a cozy place to nest. What an awful, painful death that must have been. Nothing like the happy party on the deck of the Larchmont house.

When we got back, we found some of my father's paintings had been damaged beyond repair, but others could be cleaned up with minor damage. People and wildlife, always at odds. Always competing for space and *Homo sapiens* winning, I thought.

CHAPTER 31

Il Dolce far Niente

When I was a little girl, at May Day parades in Poland I'd watch the rock doves soaring skyward on their pristine white wings, and my lungs would fill with awe and hope. I'd pick one of the flock, making its way into the blue, and watch it till it was no longer visible, imagining it had reached the highest puffy cloud where it was resting on its way to the sun.

For centuries, people have released rock doves (also known as pigeons) to mark special occasions, to commemorate milestones, to celebrate peace, and even to wage war. But by the time I became a grandmother, I had long forgotten my childhood dove fantasies. My only thought about pigeons was how to cross First Avenue in midtown Manhattan safely without getting a splat of poop on my head. There seemed to be about two-dozen pigeons always perched on the long arm of the lampposts at 55th Street, and one didn't need to be especially observant to see the swath of dried excrement on the pavement below. As a city dweller, I had become accustomed to sidestepping the dog droppings and the occasional pile of greasy MacDonald's boxes and beer cans. The pigeons were no more on my mind than the streets dug up by Con Edison crews with wide pipes in the middle of traffic lanes belching steam—at least I hoped it was steam.

But one day my granddaughters—two red-headed little girls, also Manhattan dwellers— discovered a pair of pigeons roosting on their balcony, directly in front of their bedroom window. What an amazing treat for city kids—their very own pets, but without the need for daily care!

Every morning the girls would awake to the sound of cooing and watch the birds with wide-eyed amazement before gobbling a hasty bowl of corn flakes and rushing off to school. At the science show-and-tell, they were the stars with new tales of bird observations and library research to recount in front of their envious classmates. "Maybe one of these days, you'll even see their chicks," Miss Maude, the teacher said.

"Ooh… " they said in unison. Such a possibility had never even occurred to them. They were too young to think about the birds' and the bees' private lives.

◆ ◆ ◆

One day, several months after the terrace pigeons arrived, I visited my granddaughters. As soon as I crossed the threshold, I could see by the rosy glow on their cheeks that something special was afoot.

"Bubbi, Bubbi, there are eggs in the nest!"

I hadn't seen them that excited since they got their iPods. They bombarded me with dozens of questions, which I had few answers for. Thus began a period of research and consultations with bird experts.

But while we were all excited about the impending hatchings, a nearby neighbor was hysterical.

"Get these aerial rats out of here immediately," she shouted. "Once they are settled in, you'll never be rid of them. And, oh, the piles of poop and disease! You are endangering the children!"

It was too late; the birds were already settled in. How could she have missed their romantic cooing earlier on? Obviously, not a nature lover, I thought.

For the girls, the three weeks that Mama pigeon sat on her loose nest of sticks gathered from the park across the street moved slowly, just like the car rides to the Berkshires punctuated by a constant "Are we there yet?" Right after school, the girls ran to their bedroom window to peek into the nest. They knew to keep quiet and not disturb the brooding process, but they pushed one another to get a better look and pressed their noses to the glass. They urged their mom to put out seeds and fruit each evening and delighted when the mother of a Korean schoolmate told them that having nesting pigeons in one's home bring great luck.

When the hatchlings emerged from the eggs, the excitement in the household went through the roof.

"Who knew that both parents would feed the baby birds a kind of "milk" from their throats?" the girls' father asked, astounded.

"Yes," their mom added, "and did you know the pigeon parents are paired for life?"

The awkward, initially damp nestlings depended on their parents for nearly six weeks.

♦♦♦

My granddaughters continued observing and adding pages to their show-and-tell rock dove book, which by now was approaching a pigeon encyclopedia. They researched many of the 320 species of pigeons across the world. We were all amazed that pigeons exist on every continent, because of their ability to survive in temperature extremes. From the azure-colored ones of the Indian Ocean, to yellow-footed green pigeons of the Indian Subcontinent, to a stunning array of Australian pigeons, Diamond doves, Spinifex pigeons with their unlikely erect crests, the eagle-like white-headed pigeons, bar shouldered doves, rose crowned fruit doves, African speckled pigeons, emerald-spotted wood doves, the magnificently endowed Victoria Crown pigeons and the mundane mourning doves—the species are a veritable feast for the eyes and in many cases, the palate.

Adding to their marvelous diversity, pigeons had two remarkable relatives who had gone down as sad cases of extinction in the annals of wildlife biology. The flightless dodo that used to roam the island of Mauritius, east of Madagascar, fell victim to swine and dogs brought in by European settlers. The North American Passenger pigeon, whose numbers in the millions used to blacken the skies until the early 20th century, became history when killing them for meat and feathers for ladies' hats became fashionable.

And quite apart from their biology, amazing tales of military service by courier pigeons held us spellbound. Julius Caesar, Hannibal, and Genghis Khan were all known to have used pigeons to deliver messages across enemy territory. In recent history, feathered soldiers named Cher Ami, GI Joe, Irish Paddy, and thousands of others delivered critical intelligence in World Wars I and II. Many lives were saved because essential information was carried on the backs of intrepid rock doves. All of us in the family learned a great deal about pigeons from the terrace residents.

◆ ◆ ◆

Like migratory birds, my husband and I would prepare for the annual exodus to our Florida condo as soon as the first gusts of October wind knocked the leaves off trees in New York. We would revel in the cascades of orange, yellow, and russet leaves, but just long enough to get a taste, and then we were off, anticipating sitting on our balcony facing the ocean, sipping our morning coffee and listening to the surf. Alas, the very year of our granddaughters' pigeon extravaganza, that fantasy was not to be!

We arrived weary after a three-day drive and entered our darkened apartment. The storm shutters gave the place the appearance of a cave. My husband proceeded to pull the shutters open, then called me in from another room with alarm in his voice.

"You have got to see this!"

My first thought was that he was stunned, as we always are, at the first look of the ocean vista. But that couldn't be right. Why the alarm in his voice? I hurried over and couldn't believe my eyes.

"What is *that*?"

Piles, inches of green, gray, and black balls covered the entire balcony floor.

"It looks like pigeon poop," he said, like a scientist.

"Poop! Yuck! Why?"

"They have to poop somewhere," he said, but I could see he didn't think it funny.

We'd had this condo for sixteen years, and this had never happened. Why did it happen this time? I had no idea, and my only thought was how to clean up the disaster safely, because I knew that pigeon excrement carried several deadly diseases. I ran to the computer and searched the Internet: histoplasmosis, cryptococcosis, psittacosis—all were infectious diseases that pose serious health risks. At that very moment my entire reservoir of good will toward these birds and their brethren evaporated completely. Suddenly I felt guilty about pooh-poohing the concerns of my son's next-door neighbor who feared pigeon poop. Her prediction had come to haunt *us*.

We could not step out onto the balcony until a crew in biohazard suits cleaned up the pile. But the clean-up turned out to be the least of our problems. The pigeons had moved in for good. I scoured the Internet for strategies on how to deal with the invaders who so desecrated our simple dream of seaside coffee. I found dozens of sites, and it seemed to be a massive problem many had faced before us. The array of pigeon defenses was stunning and confusing: orange balloons with big frightening eyes, plastic owls, hawks, noise-making machines, spikes made of plastic and metal. I could order these weapons online, but it would take time to have them shipped. In the meantime, we rushed out looking for large shiny Mylar balloons because we had read that the shine would frighten the birds.

On our first Sunday in Florida, we drove all over to trying to find a store that carried balloons, and when we found one we purchased a half-dozen gaudy ones and rushed home. We tied them to the balcony railings with relish and soon watched the pigeons approaching and taking a horrified pause mid-air, then backing up to settle elsewhere. We felt victorious. We congratulated ourselves on outwitting them and, exhausted, fell into the bed.

By the morning, the balloons, so plump with helium they were straining on their strings to fly skyward, had turned into flaccid imitations of themselves, drooping in surrender over the railing. Piles of fresh poop graced the floor we had painstakingly swept and scoured with Lysol *after* the cleaning company had done the initial clean-up.

"What the… " I screamed at the disgusting sight, to which my husband replied, "I told you to order that owl."

Another frantic search for pigeon warrior contractors led us to Marlin Exterminating.

"Are these the folks who spray for roaches?" my husband asked.

The next day, Marlin Exterminating installed metal spikes across the length of the balcony railings and the top of our storm door shutter case—their favorite roosting spot, apparently. It was clear that the spikes would significantly block our view of the ocean, but for the moment I didn't care. I began hallucinating about sitting contentedly on my pigeon- and poop-free balcony.

As the sky turned pinkish with the famed Florida sunset, we began watching the balcony to see what the birds, returning to their roosting perch, would do once they saw the menacing spikes. It was amazing to watch bird after bird approach the balcony and hover in the air, wings beating frantically.

"I feel like an evil landlord evicting them from their home," David said.

"Me too," I confessed.

They seemed to have a look of horror in their beady little eyes—someone has barred us from our home. Or maybe we had barred ourselves from theirs.

◆ ◆ ◆

Initially, it was immensely satisfying seeing our success, but then I began thinking. This is the trouble with thinking: one often comes to disturbing realizations. I had spent the better part of my career trying to teach not only respect for living things, but each animal's essential role in its habitat. I had taught lessons on how farmers in India contributed to the decline of tigers by killing them after claiming they devoured their livestock, or how tigers were shot by villagers frightened by their proximity. I had worked to impress on my students the need to balance animal and human needs.

And now, slowly, I began to grasp that where you stand depends entirely on where you sit. It no longer mattered to me what marvelous adaptations pigeons or doves had, how they were the stuff of rituals and cultures, how many lovely varieties there were, how they brought luck. I knew only one thing: I didn't want them sharing my balcony, just as poor Asian country folk don't want tigers roaming their backyards.

◆◆◆

After I retired from the zoo in 2007, it took me a while to absorb the fact that I had the golden opportunity to perfect *il dolce far niente*—the sweet art of doing nothing. I savored the relaxation for a few weeks. No need to wake up and wish for toothpicks to hold up my eyelids; I could scan *The New York Times* with a third cup of coffee; watch a marathon of Homeland episodes in my nightgown; organize the guest towels in my linen closet. Funny, though, how we can't escape our personalities. Just as I got antsy to return to work when my youngest was four, now I needed a project too. I'd leave the *il dolce far niente* to David. Let him become the expert. Luckily, I recovered my long-lost longing to write and plunged into poetry, then nonfiction, essays, even the inklings of a novel brewed in my brain.

A myriad of ideas percolated as I rummaged through my memory, and an unexpected scene resurfaced with such perfect clarity, I couldn't push it back. It was a vision of my young self, barely in the second year of my zoo career. There I was, seated at the head table with a starched white tablecloth in our staff dining room—a special space for senior staff—being introduced by the esteemed director himself (a privilege usually reserved for V.I.P.s like visiting scientists). I could see the amazement in the eyes of the curators: *What is she doing here? Why have we been summoned to listen to her? Education is not our thing!* I was as nervous as a chick at Easter. The big boys— and it was all men— could easily have had me for a snack.

But I had recently written up my master's thesis— research on cognitive and affective learning I had conducted on students at the zoo— and for reasons of courtesy, more than anything else, I'd sent a copy to the director. At the time, he was a towering figure in the zoo field, the inventor of the most revolutionary exhibits emulated worldwide, like the open-fronted World of Birds. Zoos in the U.S. and abroad watched his every move. I thought that as a zoologist, he'd have only a passing interest in my paper, if he ever found time to look at it, but I was wrong. He was fascinated by my study and thought it important enough for the curators to hear my main conclusion: That *affective* teaching is more important than a *cognitive* approach in changing people's attitudes.

Said another way, we needed to appeal more to the emotions, rather than just teaching the facts of science, if we wanted people to develop positive feelings toward wildlife conservation and hopefully, by extension, be willing to undertake personal actions. For the scientists, always sticklers for facts, this was an odd revelation, but the director told them that my findings had merit and may provide important breakthroughs in the future. In time, I came to understand my findings in a more personal way. It was my personal association with Carlos the puma, watching his sinuous movements, his exquisite vigilance, and those mesmerizing eyes, rather than studying cat taxonomy, morphology and all the other "-ologies", that endeared him to me and made me care about the survival of his kind and his brethren. For the zoo, the full realization of this was put into practice 25 years later with the opening of the Congo Gorilla Forest.

♦♦♦

It was this memory, mixed with the fate of my evicted pigeons, that kept surfacing every time I wanted to sit on the balcony and take in the azure waters, but decided not to because of those darn spikes in my field of vision. I had spent practically my entire career teaching the appreciation of each species' role in its environment, and here I had trouble making peace with pigeons. The farmers of India and their fear of tigers returned to my thoughts full force. Suddenly I developed more sensitive antennae for any news on the subject, and what I heard gave me a sinking feeling, as if a tsunami was about to sweep me away. In the winter of 2014, nine villagers in the province of Uttar Pradesh were eaten by tigers. At first I took it to be typical media hype, but when I saw the name of Dr. Ullas

Karanth, the eminent tiger biologist, associated with the story, I knew it was sadly, terribly true. "Human-tiger conflict is the price paid for successful tiger conservation," he said in an interview with *The New Indian Express*. The statement hit me like a powerful punch to the jaw. Indian farmers and villagers taught to appreciate the tiger lose their fear and thus can fall prey to older tigers, who are all too ready to take down a two-legged mammal. And once they develop a taste for the saltier blood of humans, they'll pass up deer or wild boar or even the leopards and bears they could sometimes take down. Chilling!

In large part due to conservation initiatives, there are now about 1,700 Bengal tigers in India (about half of all remaining tigers in the world), but the human population numbers 1.27 billion— a decidedly uneven match. That's roughly only one tiger for every 750,000 people, or a city the size of Fort Worth, Texas. And things are bound to get only more difficult for tigers as the human footprint expands. Ninety-seven percent of tigers have been wiped out in the last century. While it is tragic to think of the families who have lost a loved one to a tiger, the total extinction of the world's most iconic cats would be heartbreaking, like losing the Mona Lisa of felines. The ecosystem would suffer too: prey species—deer and wild pigs— would multiply and upset the delicate balance of nature in dwindling wild areas. So, conservation measures and the growing human population have put tigers and people on a collision course.

But recently there has been at least one glimmer of hope. In February of 2014, a group of top Indonesian clerics issued a *fatwa* that killing tigers is blasphemy, an act forbidden by God. And such an edict couldn't have come a moment too soon. Each year, hundreds of tigers are poached for their body parts for Asia's flourishing market and newly rich buyers. Every part, including claws, bones, and even whiskers is imagined to have curative properties. Small wonder that poachers can't resist the lure of the $50,000 that a single tiger can yield.

My personal solution to the Solomonic dilemmas we face when thinking of tiger conservation is to return in my thoughts to the Bronx Zoo's Tiger Mountain. Several years after it opened in 2003, I brought my grandson Michael to see it. He had been there on a Zoo Camp adventure— of course he attended— but begged me to take him there again. He couldn't get enough of the cats. I'll never forget how he stood spellbound, pressing his sunburned little nose to the glass, watching Sasha, the most curious of the cats on exhibit lunging at a deerskin, then spinning a wheel filled with hidden treats—all behavioral enrichment activities to keep the animals healthy and fit. Michael's eyes followed Sasha around the ambitious habitat with a vigilance nearly matching the cat's. His ears pricked up listening to Sasha chuffle in response to the sight of his keeper. "Is that how tigers purr?" Michael whispered.

"Yes," I replied, and wanted to say something else, but he put his index finger to his lips, signaling me to be quiet. Just then Sasha sidled up to the glass partition. Michael stood there like a stoic, unafraid of the proximity, and silently tried to count the animal's stripes. When Sasha jumped into the pool with a huge splash, Michael laughed his bell-like laugh.

That sound and the droplets of water shimmering in the summer sun are still vivid in my mind. "They are like great big pussycats, aren't they?" Michael said as we left. An old vision of Percy, Donna's proud Siamese, came to mind.

"Not exactly," I smiled, thinking of Sasha's 450-pound bulk and three-inch canines. I tugged at Michael's arm— it was past closing time—but he craned his neck, still trying to catch one last glimpse of the most powerful and beautiful cat in the world.

About the Author

Annette Libeskind Berkovits was born in Kyrgyzstan and grew up in postwar Poland and the fledgling state of Israel before coming to America at age sixteen. In her three-decade career with the Wildlife Conservation Society in New York, she spearheaded the institution's nationwide and worldwide science education programs. Her achievements include the first-ever agreement to bring environmental education to China's schools. The National Science Foundation has recognized her outstanding leadership in the field.

Now retired, she is pursuing her life-long love of writing. Her stories and poems have appeared in *Silk Road Review: a Literary Crossroads*, *Persimmon Tree* and in *American Gothic: a New Chamber Opera*. Her first memoir, *In the Unlikeliest of Places*, a story of her remarkable father's survival, was published by Wilfrid Laurier University Press in September 2014.

Also by Annette Libeskind Berkovits:

In the Unlikeliest of Places: How Nachman Libeskind Survived the Nazis, Gulags and Soviet Communism, published in 2016 by Wilfrid Laurier University Press; ISBN 978-1-77112-248-1

Reviews

"…Berkovits, Libeskind's daughter and the author of this cinematically gripping debut biography, does a masterful job weaving together a coherent narrative, culled largely from tape recordings that her father left behind. She has a rare gift for storytelling… the prose is lively and direct, and the story is deeply affecting… A moving tale that's emotionally powerful and historically edifying."

—Kirkus Reviews

"…an incandescent biographical tribute to the author's father, Nachman Libeskind, an eternally hopeful survivor… Berkovits traces such challenges (as maintaining one's Judaism after the Holocaust) though her generation and the next, and this journey—a story within a story—warrants attention and reflection…some of Nachman's art is included late in the book, adding dimensionality to a text already replete with it. …Though this is, inescapably, a Holocaust survivor's biography, it is not dominated by those horrors; rather, it celebrates the ingenuity with which one man made his time less about enduring than about living vibrantly."

—Clarion Foreword Review

"This is a book that works on so many levels: as the biography of a Polish Jew who narrowly escapes two murderous totalitarian systems, as a personal journey that leads to a new life in the United States marked by optimism and accomplishment—and, above all, as the beautiful, heartfelt tribute of a daughter to her remarkable father."

—Andrew Nagorski, author of
Hitlerland: American Eyewitnesses
to the Nazi Rise to Power **(2012)**

You can learn more about the author and her writing on **annetteberkovits.com**

42058070R00202

Made in the USA
Middletown, DE
31 March 2017